Development Planning and Structural Inequalities

Development Planning and Structural Inequalities

The Response of the Underprivileged

VICTOR S. D'SOUZA

SAGE PUBLICATIONS
New Delhi/Newbury Park/London

First published in 1990 by
Sage Publications India Pvt Ltd
32, M–Block Market, Greater Kailash I
New Delhi 110 048

Sage Publications Inc
2111 Hillcrest Drive
Newbury Park, California 91320

Sage Publications Ltd
6 Bonhill Street
London EC 2A 4PU

Published by Tejeshwar Singh for Sage Publications India Pvt. Ltd, phototypeset by Mudra Typesetters, Pondicherry and printed at Chaman Offset Printers.

Library of Congress Cataloging-in-Publication Data

D'Souza, Victor Salvadore, 1923-
    Development planning and structural inequalities : the response of
the underprivileged / Victor S. D'Souza.
        p.   cm.
    Includes bibliographical references (p.).
    1. Social structure—India. 2. Untouchables. 3. India—Scheduled tribes.
4. India—Economic policy—1947- 5. India—Economic conditions—1947-
6. India—Social policy. 7. India—Social conditions—1947- I. Title.
HN683.5.D76   1990   305.5' 0954—dc20   90-9040

ISBN: 0–8039–9664–0
        81–7036–209–1

Contents

List of Tables

Acknowledgements

The theme of this study springs from my abiding interest in the sociological aspects of inequality and development. The study itself was made possible by the generous offer of a National Fellowship by the Indian Council of Social Science Research. In expressing my gratitude to the ICSSR, I recall with pleasure the many courtesies I have received from its successive Chairmen— G. Parthasarathy and Prof. S. Chakravarty—and Member-Secretaries—Prof. D.D. Narula and Prof. Iqbal Narain—and their staff.

Working facilities during my National Fellowship were graciously extended by Prof. M.S. Gore, Vice-Chancellor, and Prof. D. Narain, at the Department of Sociology, University of Bombay. Similarly, Dr S.D. Karnik placed at my disposal the facilities of the ICSSR Western Regional Centre in Bombay.

Several persons and institutions alleviated the tediousness involved in an empirical investigation, especially Ulhas D'Souza who did the computer-processing of data; the Bombay Suburban Electricity Supply Limited gave, free of charge, their valuable computer time. Last but not least, I am indebted to my wife, Priscilla, for bearing with me cheerfully while I was preoccupied with the study.

Whereas I am entirely responsible for the many shortcomings, and acts of commission and omission, which a work of this type, using available data, is bound to contain, I must say with gratefulness that I benefited immensely from the comments by Prof. M.S. Gore and by the publisher's referee in preparing the final typescript.

June 1990   VICTOR S. D'SOUZA

1

Development Planning and Social Transformation

The Concept of Development

The concept of development owes its currency to the idea of universal progress put forward in the writings of the Enlightenment thinkers. Reacting to the rapid changes in the society of their time, and sensing the shape of things to come, the philosophers of the eighteenth century proclaimed the emergence of a new social order based on the principles of liberty, equality and fraternity. These ideas strongly influenced the theoretical perspectives of the various social sciences which came to be established soon after, with the objective of finding solutions to the problems of rapid social change.

A major cause of the rapid social change was the industrial revolution. Although the industrial revolution is an aspect of economic development, its impact on the social life of the people, leading to far-reaching changes in society, soon became evident. Therefore, it was thought that the process of industrialization would bring about a fundamental transformation in society, thereby associating progress and development with industrialism or economic development.

As the industrial revolution was gaining ground, two major social philosophical ideas about man's happiness and social good were formulated during the latter part of the nineteenth century. The first idea, forming part of the philosophical system of utilitarianism propounded by Jeremy Bentham, maintained that man's happiness lies in the maximization of utilities so that through his material possessions he can fulfil all his needs including the non-material ones. The other idea, which owes its philosophical formulation to John Stuart Mill, emphasized that man's happiness and social good depended on the maximization of man's capacities rather than of the utilities. In this view, man's being and dignity are given more importance than his possessions (Randall, 1965: 589–636). It is, however, the idea of the maximization of utilities which was in full accord with the industrial revolution, which gained ascendency during the first phase of thinking on development planning. This idea, in fact, reinforced the faith in industrialism as the harbinger of human progress.

Various social scientists (including even sociologists) lent credibility to the above assumption by formulating theories of modernization which dealt with the process of social transformation brought about by industrialization. It was suggested that there was a logic or imperative to industrial systems. This was derived from the technology and efficiency, characteristic of these systems, which produced a congruence or uniformity of thinking and behaviour among people, which tended to cut across national and cultural boundaries. The distinctive personality type emerging from the exposure to industrialism is termed the *individual modernity syndrome*, and the individual with such a personality is called the 'industrial man'. The industrial man possesses traits such as efficiency, control over nature, planning ahead, openness to new experience, tolerance of diversity, and active citizenship (Inkeles, 1960). In a cross-national study covering six countries—Argentina, Chile, Bangladesh, India, Israel and Nigeria—it was demonstrated that people exposed to industrialization in these countries tended to have similar clusters of attitudes approximating to the individual modernity syndrome, despite marked variations in underlying cultures (Inkeles and Smith, 1974).

The model of economic development systematized by W.W. Rostow (1961), gained immediate currency. According to this model, development is a linear process; therefore, in their advancement, the underdeveloped countries have to traverse the same steps that the countries, which are now in the vanguard of economic progress, had gone through. In Rostow's opinion, the capitalist countries, such as the United States, have attained the highest stage of development, and the Third World countries, which are at a lower stage, have to catch up with the former if they are to develop.

One of the major planks in the fight for independence of the former colonial countries, including India, was the claim that once they were free from the shackles of foreign domination, they could undertake the task of development by reconstructing their economies and restructuring their societies When they were actually free, they hardly needed to be convinced that in order to bring about development, all that they had to do was to trace the steps of the developed Western countries, as suggested by Rostow, by undertaking economic development through industrialization. Accordingly, most of the newly independent countries embarked upon ambitious programmes of development planning. Whereas economic development has been the major focus of planning, the ultimate objective is to bring about a transformation in the society towards the fulfilment of the goals of a just society. In this the developing countries were encouraged by the United Nations by its declaration of Development Decades. However, soon afterwards, the results of economic development were all there for everyone to see.

In India, there have been some remarkable achievements of economic development, such as the transformation of the agricultural economy and the attainment of self-sufficiency in food. Even though the growth rates of the economy, in general, have not come up to expectations, they have more than kept pace with the phenomenal growth of population. But the impact of economic development on the social structure has been disappointing (Chakravarty, 1987: 88–89). Indeed, economic development has also affected social structure, but mainly in directions opposite to the desired ones. For example, the traditional Indian social structure is characterized by social exclusivism and glaring inequalities; but, despite expectations to the contrary, development planning has widened the inequalities, and sharpened further the divisive tendencies. The faith in economic development as an efficient means to bring about social transformation of the desired kind has been seriously shaken.

The disenchantment with economic development is not confined to the developing societies alone. It is even more pronounced in the developed societies of the West where economic development has released forces which have resulted in a series of crises, such as structural unemployment compounded by the unequal distribution of working opportunities among sexes, ages, classes and ethnic groups; mounting costs and excessive bureaucratization of welfare services created to take care of the unemployed and the deprived, rendering the measures increasingly self-defeating; growing irrelevance of the educational system which fails to equip people to cope with the complex problems of life; high levels of consumption, leading to inordinate wastefulness of people's time and of natural resources; lethal levels of environmental pollution and the ever-present threat of nuclear annihilation (Sachs, 1978). Because of these crises, the unprecedented growth of the richer countries, instead of enabling their people to lead a life of self-fulfilment, has driven large sections of their population to resort to what is termed the 'chemical way of life', just to be able to cope with the complexity of their living conditions. Such overwhelming gloom under a pall of glitter has impelled perceptive observers to redesignate so-called development 'maldevelopment' in the advanced countries (Galtung *et al.*, 1982).

In fact, the encouragement of the developmental efforts of the Third World countries by the United Nations, through the declaration of Development Decades, also led to a reassessment of the concept of development. Although the First Development Decade took for granted the theory of narrow economic development which arose in the West during the 1950s and the 1960s (especially the Rostow model), towards end of the First and during the Second Development Decade a debate started in a number of United Nations bodies and institutions expressing a desire to break away from the original concept (UNESCO, 1982: 1–68). The debate tore apart the concept of linear development and laid bare the pitfalls in Rostow's model of successive stages of development. The emphasis shifted from purely economic development to integrated development, which called attention to the interaction of the environmental, technical, economic and social aspects of the development process.

In the process of questioning and in the transformation of the old concept of development, a fundamental change in the underlying philosophical premise of development has also occurred. Instead of the maximization of utilities as the basis of social good and development, it is now recognized that the basis of development should be the maximization of human capacities. This idea, which was put forward by John Stuart Mill, has lately been popularized by Erich Fromm (1979). Now, in order to distinguish from the old concept of development, the emerging concept is described as 'development centred on the human being' (Galtung *et al.*, 1982) or 'development centred on man' (Loubser, 1982).

Development centred on the human being has many radical implications, including a new way of life as described by Fromm, Galtung and the others. In particular, it refers to a multifaceted socio-cultural transformation, the satisfaction of the basic needs of every person, at the least, special efforts at uplifting the depressed masses, and the mobilization of the resources of the people themselves in a self-reliant fashion.

The dominant goal, according to the concept of development centred on the human being, is to provide opportunities of self-realization to every individual and in every society. The concept of the developed individual has also undergone a change: a developed person is different from the 'industrial man' or the 'modern man' who is said to have the characteristics which are necessary to function in an industrial society. The system of personality which a developed individual should have is termed the *ego development syndrome*. In ego development a person moves from an impulsive, narrow, self-centred being to a richly multifaceted, mature, autonomous and sympathetic person. A developed person is self-reliant, creative and sociable. True development lies in enabling a person to live *to be* rather than to live *to have* (Lagos, 1975, Fromm, 1979).

Insofar as the individual and the society are interrelated, development calls for a particular pattern of society, of which the society characterised by the ideals of liberty, equality and freedom would appear to be a suitable model. A developed society should provide the individual with the freedom of choice, equality of opportunity and the chance of mixing freely in society.

These visions of the developed individual and the developed society are ultimately derived from the goal of development, which is based on moral values which are an aspect of culture. However, it goes without saying that no worthwhile development is possible without a certain degree of economic development. But unless the value premises of development are kept in view, economic development would only enable a person to live *to have* which is sheer avarice, rather than to live *to be* which is self-fulfilment. Therefore, in the ultimate analysis, the idea of development is embedded in moral values, and not in the economic matrix. Development is thus a complex variable with psychological, social, economic and cultural dimensions. But, in their interrelationships, the cultural or moral values have primacy over the other dimensions; for it is the values which have to motivate and guide the restructuring of the economy and the society for the self-realization of individuals.

In fact, all planning is based on certain value premises. There are at least three major types of value perspectives, underlying development planning—conservative, liberal and radical. The conservative value perspective assumes that a given social order is wholesome and sacrosanct, having a vitality of its own and, therefore, should not be unduly disturbed. However, planning may be resorted to stimulate the growth of the economy and to iron out the rough edges of the time-tested societal devices such as the market mechanism in the modern society.

The liberal value perspective, on the other hand, takes into account the deep-seated injustices and malfunctioning that may be widespread in a society. It aims at bringing about an evolutionary transformation in the society through reformist planning, even by changing some of the institutional structures. The radical value perspective is similar to the liberal one, insofar as both recognize the unjust nature of the historically evolved societies, and the need for their transformation. But the former differs from the latter in advocating a complete restructuring of the society, preceded by a revolution, violence notwithstanding. The three major forms of planning corresponding to their intended impact on the political systems—whether maintenance, evolutionary change or structural transformation—are identified as allocative, innovative and radical respectively (Friedmann 1987: 47).

However, apart from the conservative value perspective, even the planning undertaken by the liberal democracies and the socialist societies (which have followed the liberal and radical value perspectives respectively) has not succeeded in bringing about transformation either in the personality system or in the social system, as envisaged by the concept of development. Interestingly, despite qualitative differences in their value perspectives, both the liberal democracies and socialist societies have employed industrialization and economic development as instruments of social transformation. It is true that both the systems have succeeded in achieving higher levels of economic growth but, so far as the transformation of their societies is concerned, they have achieved only partial success, and that too in different directions. By and large, the liberal democracies have achieved a great degree of freedom for their citizens, but at the cost of increasing inequalities (except perhaps in some of the Scandinavian countries). On the other hand, the socialist societies have succeeded in achieving a greater degree of equality among their members, but it is at the expense of individual freedom. Moreover, in neither type of society has any serious attempt been made to foster the feeling of mutual concern among the people (with rare exceptions, such as Kim Il Sung's Korea). If social exclusivism based on narrow, primordial ties has been weakened in both the types of societies, it has not been replaced by social inclusivism of universal concern. The result is that individuals have become more and more indifferent towards one another. Both types of societies would be found wanting in their capacity to bring about well-rounded development among their members.

Shortcomings of Development Planning in India

Without attempting a critique of development planning in India, only a few significant shortcomings of planning will be dealt with here in the light of the preceding discussion on the nature of development. The struggle for independence in India was fought with the ideals of the Enlightenment and the moral imperatives of a *Ram-rajya* as interpreted by Mahatma Gandhi. The values of freedom, equality and fraternity, and compassion for the under-privileged are enshrined in the Constitution of free India, with directives to the governments to actualize them. Planning in India, therefore, is a sequel to the directive principles of the Constitution which aim at a socialistic transformation of the Indian society. The governments of India, however, have opted for an innovative and evolutionary rather than a radical and revolutionary way of bringing about social transformation. Therefore, the value perspective underlying Indian planning may be broadly labelled as that of the liberal variety.

However, in practice, it is pragmatism which has guided the course of planning in India, aimed at achieving quick economic results. Although, in keeping with the socialistic ideals, a mixed economy was instituted by creating a series of public enterprises to complement the private organizations, the economy has been functioning mainly on capitalist lines, with public enterprises often subserving private interests. The organization of the economy with private ownership of the means of production, profit as the prime motive for setting up economic enterprises, and competition as the chief mode of economic striving, only helps a few powerful individuals in their self-aggrandizement, to the detriment of the common man. When the economy grows, such a mode of production only leads to the rich growing richer and the poor remaining where they were, resulting in widening economic disparities among the people.

True development, on the other hand, depends upon economic growth as well as equitable distribution. This can be accomplished only if ownership of the means of production is subjected to social responsibilities, the avaricious profit motive is tempered with a concern for the welfare and interest of others and, without jeopardizing efficiency, competition is replaced with cooperation. In other words, the driving force of self-interest in economic activity should be replaced with that of altruism. This is not an impossible task if people are made to realize how much they owe their achievement and success to the contributions of the others in society as well as to the labour of past generations; they would then recognize their responsibility to others as well as to the future generations. In any case, by and large, an individual has greater concern for one's near and dear ones than for oneself. Development means the extension of this concern to wider circles. However, emphasis on economic development alone, which diminishes the bonds of human reciprocity, erodes one's concern even for one's close ones, and renders one more and more selfish. This is what has been happening in India in the name of development.

Despite the need to undertake a radical reconstruction of the economic organization, consistent with the goals of development, the priorities and strategies of planning adopted have tended to favour the interests of the dominant sections. To begin with, economic development as such was made the focus of planning. To justify this, it was argued that without substantial economic development no real improvement in the lot of the underprivileged sections was possible. The size of the pie was so small that its redistribution—by depriving a small privileged section—would not materially advance the well-being of the poor multitudes. Therefore, in order to improve the condition of the underprivileged, it was initially decided to increase the size of the pie rather than to change the way it was cut. Thus, the development of the economy became the sheet-anchor of Indian planning, and the growth rate of the economy became the yardstick for measuring the success of planning. Despite the repeated emphasis in every plan that the transformation of society is an even greater objective of planning, the issues of social justice have received only scant attention by planners, with the provision of only symbolic measures for their realization.

With a view to inducing rapid economic development, a strategy of global planning has been employed. This brings about overall economic development by first introducing changes in the potentially rich regions and among people with resources who are more receptive to change. The strategy of global planning has resulted in reinforcing the production capacities of people who are economically already advanced. This is not an unintended consequence, but one which has been promoted by design, in the hope that the economic gains made by the upper echelons would trickle down to the bottom layers of the society. The trickle down effect has occurred. However, what was not anticipated was that while both the ceiling and the floor have risen, the ceiling has risen faster than the floor, so that the inequalities have widened further and the lower strata have benefited only marginally.

The priorities and strategies adopted in planning have resulted in serious anomalies in the results attained. Witness, for example, the phenomenal success in increasing food production in the country in general, and in certain regions in particular. The owner-cultivators and the traders in the country have benefited immensely from this. However, despite the fact that the granaries are overflowing and food is rotting in the godowns, millions in the country are starving and malnutritioned. What has happened to the hope that once the country becomes self-sufficient in food, the problem of hunger and malnutrition would be contained? It only shows that equitable distribution has nothing to do with the size of the resources. For the way the pie is cut does not depend upon the size of the pie but, in this case, upon the social structure. If the social structure is basically unequal, the distribution is bound to be inequitable as well, whether the pie is large or small.

True development, among other things, lies in improving the productive capacities of the underprivileged sections. On the contrary, under the prevailing scheme of development planning aimed at rapid economic growth by employing sophisticated technologies, it is only the productive capacities of the economically developed classes that are improving, even at the expense of displacing the underprivileged from their employment, however underpaid they may be. From a state of oppression, those living on the margin of subsistence are reduced to a state of uselessness.

These are only illustrations to show that the problems of social justice cannot be resolved and the goal of the well-rounded development of every individual cannot be fulfilled by economic planning alone. For, the problems and issues of this nature are lodged in the social structure. On the other hand, the social structure has also a reality and independence of its own and, therefore, it also has the capacity to channel the changes in the economy to reinforce itself. So far, development planners, notwithstanding their different ideological positions, have considered social structure mainly as an epiphenomenon of the economic structure.

Resilience of the Social Structure

This study emphasizes the resilience of the social structure. It illustrates how the social structure has been able to channel the effects of economic development so as to maintain its basic pattern, which is anti-development.

Just as the concept of development has undergone a metamorphosis in response to the changing experience of development planning, there is also a need to re-analyse the concept of social structure commensurate with the new meaning of development. The popular conceptions of social structure are hardly able to deal with the fresh issues of development, as they were formulated much before the emergence of the new concept of development. This can be illustrated with two examples—one from a specific concept of social structure applicable to the Indian society and the other from a general concept.

The social structure of the Indian society is usually described in terms of its major elements—the joint family, the caste system and the village community. It is presumed and actually confirmed by studies that when economic development takes place (say, through industrialization), the joint family yields to the nuclear pattern, the immobile caste system to the mobile class system, and the relatively isolated village community gets itself more integrated with its wider region. At best, this description of the social structure is suited to deal with changes due to modernization and cannot throw light upon the model of a developed society. It also cannot account for the resilience of the social structure.

In more general terms, social structure is usually regarded as consisting of three basic elements- -position, role and status. Such a conceptualization is ideal to bring out the interrelationship between the social structure and economy. However, it has its own limitations in dealing with the concept of development.

The intimate relationship between the social structure and the economic structure can be easily seen if it is recognized that both these structures intersect in the variable of occupational prestige. The occupations are generated by the division of labour in the economy; on the other hand, for the most part, the position, role and status of members (units) in the social structure are derived from their occupations. Therefore, any change in the occupational structure, will have repercussions which will affect the social structure as well.

For example, when an agricultural economy (with its informal organization and with the household as the unit of production) changes into an industrial economy (with its formal organization depriving the household of its production function), far-reaching changes are known to take place in the relationships between the members of different sexes and of generations, in the structure of the family and in the social stratification system. Changes of this kind may give the impression that in the relationship between the social structure and the economic structure, the latter is the independent variable and the former, the dependent one. From this it would follow that any far-reaching transformation in the economy (such as, industrialization) could turn the society inside out. Indeed, this is the assumption underlying the concept of modernization which attributes a whole range of changes in society, culture and personality to the process of industrialization. Such a conceptualization, however, totally ignores the possibility of the social structure having an autonomy of its own and the fact of its resilience.

In order to understand the relationship between social structure and development, the concept of social structure should answer the following three questions: What is the ideal-typical social

structure of a developed society? What are the unjust and problematic features of our existing society? How does an unjust social
structure perpetuate itself? It is on the basis of the answers that
one can decide whether economic or industrial development alone
can bring about the transformation of the social structure in the
desired direction.

In formulating the concept of social structure here, I would like
to take as my point of departure the distinction made by Raymond
Firth between social structure and social organization (Firth, 1964:
57–58). Speaking about the simpler societies, Firth defined social
structure as the model of the basic elements of society representing
the expected pattern of behaviour, which is pervasive and relatively
long persisting. Social organization, on the other hand, is the
process of ordering action and relations in reference to given social
ends, and in terms of adjustments resulting from the exercise of
choices by the members of the society. Social organization also has
its particular behaviour pattern which is formed out of the elements
drawn from the social structure, but which are modified, altered or
replaced according to the needs of the social organization. The
modified or newly inducted elements in the social organization
eventually become part of the social structure. Thus, there is
constant interaction between social structure and social organization, each influencing the other.

Both social structure and social organization are patterns of
social relationships and hence have aspects of groups. Speaking of
complex societies, social structure can be distinguished as made up
of loosely organized groupings with diffused goals, formed on the
basis of certain background characteristics of members, which are
often permanent and socially inherited. Social organization, on the
other hand, can be identified with relatively more tightly organized
groups aimed at fulfilling specific goals. The various economic
enterprises and administrative and voluntary bodies, in which
means-ends relationships are clearly articulated, can be regarded
as examples of social organization. The basic distinction between
social structure and social organization, as one can see from this
formulation, is that whereas the groupings forming the social
structure are sustained by certain characteristics of the members,
social organizations are sustained by their goals. That is why the
groupings in the social structure are relatively more pervasive and
lasting as compared to social organizations which are relatively

more specific and ephemeral. It may also be mentioned that in a broad sense, social organizations give rise to basically instrumental behaviour, which is behaviour governed by goals, whereas the groupings in the social structure give scope for expressive behaviour in which behaviour is an end in itself.

Let us have a closer look at the groupings in social structure. All social groups are made up of social relations which represent certain kinds of glues or ties, binding people together. Sociologists and social psychologists usually refer to two different kinds of relational dimensions underlying group formation: the dimension of power and the dimension of affiliation.

The dimension of power refers to the role relationships among people which are based on a differential distribution of economic and political power. Since the dimension of power orders the various groups into a hierarchy of superior–subordinate relationships, it may be termed the hierarchical dimension. The class system, based on an unequal distribution of social, economic and political power, is an appropriate example of hierarchical groupings.

The dimension of affiliation refers to the relationship of affect or feeling. Certain kinds of groups are characterised by a strong sense of solidarity among its members. On the other hand, the different groups of this category tend to be indifferent or even antagonistic towards one another. Social scientists have devised scales and indices to measure the social distance among such groups. The social distance corresponds to the continuum of affiliation—ranging from an extreme degree of liking to the extreme degree of dislike, or from an extreme degree of concern to an extreme degree of unconcern.

Usually groupings based on cultural bonds (such as, ethnic, religious and linguistic ties) generate a sense of solidarity among their members. The religious grouping is especially important among the affiliational groupings, as religion not only forges a strong bond of fellowship among its members but also sacralizes their self-identity so that they feel a strong sense of loyalty to the group.

As already mentioned, one is usually born into one's groupings in the social structure. While this is especially true in the case of affiliational groupings, mobility is often possible in hierarchical groupings such as classes.

A third dimension of group formation, which is seldom studied by sociologists, is space. Identity of interests, socio-cultural similarity and spatial propinquity are important determinants of social interaction. Other things being equal, those who live closer together interact with one another more than those who live farther apart. For example, the neighbourhood is an important social category with a strong spatial connotation. Another important aspect of space which has a bearing on social relationships is what is termed the 'territorial imperative' (Ardery, 1966). This is an impulse which humans share with some species of the animal and bird kingdoms, because of which a social group inhabiting a given geographical area tends to claim sovereignty over that area. While the spatial aspect of groupings is especially important in tribal societies, it is assuming greater importance in the non-tribal areas as well, with the accelerating processes of migration and urbanization.

Social scientists are aware of the different relational dimensions and the groupings based on them. However, in their analyses, they tend to deal with each type of grouping separately; further, the different types of groupings have been dealt with by specialists in different fields. For example, hierarchical groupings are considered when dealing with the political economy and social stratification, affiliational groupings in studies in social psychology and ethnic relations, and territorial groupings in urban studies. Because of their exclusive treatment, the issues stemming from the interrelationships of the various categories of groupings have not received sufficient attention.

Social structure, on the other hand, stands for the interrelationships among the different categories of groupings—hierarchical, affiliational and territorial. However, most of the analyses of social structure, especially those using the elements of position, role and status, and the Marxist perspective, confine themselves to the hierarchical groupings alone. They, therefore, fail to take note of the complexity and the vital forces inherent in the social structure.

Each of the relational dimensions, with the social groupings based on it, has its own importance for the individual and the society. Through his position in the hierarchical dimension, particularly through his occupational role, he relates himself usually to the rest of society. The affiliational groupings nurture the altruistic qualities (such as, devotion, sympathy, love and concern for one another) which lubricate the wheels of social life; they also fulfil the individual's need for sociability and emotional satisfaction. The territorial groupings lend support and stability to socio-cultural life. Above all, as already pointed out, these groupings in the social structure foster expressive behaviour which is necessary for satisfying the higher order needs of individuals, such as love, dignity and self-actualization.

Whereas the different social structural groupings have their respective positive roles to play in the society, they become problematic when the domains of the different types of groupings invade one another's territory. Thus, it is very often found that the occupational roles and political power, which belong to the domain of the hierarchical groupings, are channelled through the affiliational and territorial groupings. As a result of this phenomenon, the social, economic and political disparities existing between groups become permanently established and social inequalities become rigid and unalterable. This would appear to be the principal structural basis for the perpetuation of inequalities in society (D'Souza, 1981). There are innumerable examples in history of how some of the dominant groups have manipulated the institutional structures so that whatever the changes, they would always remain at the top.

Even when there are no formal institutional arrangements to favour the more powerful groupings, the social structure has forces within itself which would ensure almost the same result. If the members of a powerful grouping also belong to the same affiliational or territorial grouping because of their affective ties, they are prone to reinforce one another's privileges. On the other hand, the members of a disadvantaged grouping, because of their lack of affective ties with influential persons, are left to live in a perpetual state of misery. That is why, in India, the people now designated as the Scheduled Castes and the Scheduled Tribes, who do not have the empathetic support of the dominant castes, have been economically and politically deprived for centuries.

Development as Social Transformation

One of the important features of traditional and undeveloped societies is that the three relational dimensions of power, affective ties and territorial ties interpenetrate in the same grouping. Such societies are characterized by social exclusivism, social inequalities and lack of freedom for the individual. Development would consist of unscrambling the relational dimensions and restoring to each category of groupings its legitimate domain.

Economic development by itself would not be capable of bringing about the societal transformation envisaged above. On the contrary, at least in the initial stages of economic development, the fruits of economic development are also likely to be channelled through the social structure, the richer sections getting the lion's share. Consequently, the inequalities would widen.

The economically developed countries present yet another kind of picture of maldevelopment. Since economic development directly influences occupational roles, it has greatly enhanced the importance of role relationships or the dimension of power. Correspondingly, the importance of affective and territorial ties has been downgraded. Accordingly, the influence of religious and ethnic grouping has become weaker, and neighbours have become strangers. Francis Hsu, a leading social psychologist, has drawn attention to the erosion of affective ties in American society due to the onslaught of the occupational role, and its implications for the society. The erosion has taken place at the fountainhead of affective qualities. Family and kinship, which play a major part in the generation and nurturing of affective impulses, hold the key to social and cultural development. The source having become weaker, the communitarian aspects of social life (concern for one another and inner social control) have diminished, thereby necessitating strong measures of outer control to maintain law and order (Hsu, 1977).

Affective impulses, besides being the mainspring of individual action, are the cementing bond of a healthy society in which self-fulfilment is possible. True development requires that affective ties must be strengthened; in addition, the concern which one expresses for one's near and dear ones has to be extended to wider networks. In other words, individuals have to be socialized into persons with a wider empathy.

Development (of the kind in which people entertain broader sympathies embracing the wider society) certainly requires social transformation of the type in which the economic and political roles of the affiliational and territorial groupings are curbed.

However, ideally, the curbing of their economic and political roles should not result in a weakening or disappearance of these groupings, for they have their other legitimate roles to play in the society. What is needed is a transcendence of the affiliational and territorial ties. The nature of such a transcendence can be illustrated with the celebrated example of Mahatma Gandhi who, depsite his deep-seated Hindu identity, was equally concerned about people of all religions.

To conclude, the crux of the new approach to development lies in the fact that whereas in economic development one hopes for the emergence of the desired type of person as a result of industrialism, in development focused on the human being, one changes the economic and social structure in a manner conducive to the emergence of the desired type of person. The new approach does not represent a negation of industrialism or economic development; rather, it stresses that instead of the man subserving the economy, the latter should subserve the former. According to development centred on man, most of the problems faced by man are the result of faulty economic and social structures. As things stand, rather than these structures being continually adapted for the self-fulfilment of individuals, it is the latter who are required to adapt themselves to the changes in the former. Man, therefore, constantly sways with the onslaught of economic and political changes and becomes a victim of his circumstances. How does an iniquitous social structure hold its own despite economic change and growth will be illustrated in subsequent chapters.

In this study, the analysis is undoubtedly oriented to the concept of development centred on the human being. Therefore, issues such as the transformation of the unjust social structure, the removal of glaring inequalities in the society, and the concern for the development of the underprivileged assume paramount importance in evaluating the outcome of planned development. Accordingly, in Chapter 2, by making use of the findings of the available studies, it has been shown that, by and large, the changes generated by economic development have been channelled through the existing social structure. There are a wide variety of contexts in which changes have occurred, but in every case the change is governed by one or another aspect of the social structure. The result is a further distortion of the social structure, which exacerbates the inequities and tension in the society.

In Chapter 3, the problem of the growing inequalities among the Scheduled Castes themselves has been systematically analysed. The analysis reveals how the spatial and social structural aspects combine to accentuate inequalities when growth takes place.

Chapters 4, 5 and 6 deal with the changes in the three crucial dimensions—education, urbanization and industrialization—of the two major underprivileged sections of the Indian society, namely, the Scheduled Castes and the Scheduled Tribes, covering a period of about twenty years of planned development. Analysing data taken from the 1961, 1971 and 1981 Census publications, the patterns of absolute and relative growth of these population categories are examined. Particular attention has been paid to their relative growth, which has to do with the inequalities in society and the transformation of the social structure. The analysis is aimed at examining whether the pattern of development of the Scheduled Castes and the Scheduled Tribes is in keeping with the general growth pattern or is influenced by features of the social structure.

Although the use of census data for understanding the problem of development has its own limitations, the study has been reinforced by analysing data at two levels: first, the country is treated as the universe with the larger states as the units; and, second, each of the states is treated as the universe with its districts as units. The two sets of results in this case support each other.

Finally, an attempt has been made to draw the implications of the findings for a planning strategy geared to the developmental problem of the underprivileged.

2

Social Mobility and Social Transformation: Some Prevailing Trends

Social Change and Social Transformation

In the final analysis, social development has to be brought about through social change or social transformation. However, social change is a continual process, although the tempo of change varies. In the past, the change in a society was so small and gradual that a given social order appeared to be a permanent one; but, in recent times, social change has become so rapid that it gives the impression that society is chaotic. Thus, the theme of social change has become complex and confusing. It is, therefore, necessary to view this subject with the help of some general guidelines.

Social change has been viewed from different analytical perspectives. These have resulted in different grand formulations—such as, the classical evolutionary, cyclical, functional and conflict theories of change. Such grand theories are not only at variance with one another but they have also been found to be wanting when put to test in the study of real situations. One of the common underlying principles of all these theories is the idea of determinism which is now being discarded in almost every scientific discipline. These theories have, therefore, been subjected to a reappraisal by several authors. Some of the ideas emerging from such discussions (see, especially, Moore, 1960; Parsons, 1964; and Eisenstadt, 1964), may be advantageously employed in analysing the Indian situation.

Some ideas about social change which are relevant for our analysis now follow. Apart from the exogenous sources of change, tendencies for change are inherent in all societies. No society is completely integrated, although integration is necessary for normal social life. And, even in a well-integrated society, there are sets of dialectic factors which generate strain, making for change. Not all changes call for or result in a change in the social structure. Social structural changes are brought about by changes that result in differentiation, which is a process whereby the units become more and more autonomous as well as interdependent. Differentiation loosens the existing integration and calls for reintegration through the institutionalization of change. But, unlike the assumptions of the classical theorists, reintegration of society is neither automatic nor does it assume a predictable form. Also, reintegration following differentiation does not necessarily represent a higher stage of development. Reintegration may even lead to regression or, still worse, disintegration. Voluntary and planned effort is especially called for in institutionalizing change and reintegrating society in a desired direction. It may be added that the use of value-loaded terms is unavoidable when discussing social change and development.

The unfolding results of industrialization and economic development are in accord with the revised views about social change. Although industrialization has brought about differentiation which is characterized by the processes of modernization, the reintegration that has taken place in many developed societies, as discussed in the previous chapter, has not resulted in a desired stage of development or progress. The industrial and even post-industrial societies have not succeeded in directing social changes in the desired direction.

One of the major aspects of social transformation to promote development is to bring about a redistribution of social, economic and political power in the society, for, an underdeveloped society is usually characterized by rigid inequalities. This process can be better understood in terms of the redistribution of occupations which are a major source of inequalities. From the standpoint of occupational distribution, there are three major aspects involved in social inequalities: social differentiation of positions (occupations) based on the division of labour in society; the ranking of positions resulting in a status hierarchy; and the tendency for the intergenerational perpetuation of positions, or the principle of status ascription. All these aspects have different magnitudes in economically developed and underdeveloped societies. For example, occupational differentiation is far more complex in an economically developed than in an underdeveloped society. The tendency for the intergenerational perpetuation of occupations is especially strong in underdeveloped societies. In truly developed societies there ought to be not only a higher degree of equality of opportunity, but also a greater degree of egalitarianism even when there are differences in status and authority.

Poverty Alleviation versus Mobility

Economists usually abstract the economic-value component of occupations and analyse inequalities in terms of income and assets of the members of the society. Analysts of income and assets distribution in society have focused attention mainly on the pattern of inequality in the distribution of income and assets as well as poverty which is the lower extremity of that pattern. In other words, economists are concerned only with the second of the major aspects of inequality, namely the hierarchical distribution of status and income, and stop short of the major goal of development—to get rid of the tendency for the intergenerational perpetuation of inequalities. Even so, the economic analysis of poverty and income distribution has made an important contribution to our understanding of social inequalities.

However, the aspect of the pattern of inequalities which has received considerable attention in development planning in India, especially in the Sixth and Seventh Five Year Plans, is the problem of poverty in the wake of exhaustive analysis by economists (Dandekar and Rath, 1971) which had drawn attention to the growing enormity of this problem. There are now several schemes aimed at poverty alleviation and the Planning Commission has claimed that the percentage of population in India below the poverty line has come down from 48.3 in 1978–79 to 36.9 in 1984–85. This percentage has been projected to come down further to 25.8 by 1989–90 (*Seventh Five Year Plan*, Vol. I, p. 33).

Apart from poverty, the phenomenon of unequal income distribution gives rise to a number of other problems in society, making for tension and conflict. This broader issue of the pattern of inequality has not received much attention on the part of Indian planners—a fact bemoaned by Dantwala (1987). Quoting various authorities, Dantwala has pointed out that there is extreme inequality in the ownership of assets—whereas 40 per cent of the households at the bottom had assets worth only 4.3 per cent of the total value, a small minority (8.4 per cent) of the households, each owning assets of one lakh and above, cornered 48.4 per cent of the total assets in 1981–82 (NSS 37th Round). Again, according to him, the skewed distribution of assets has remained almost the same since the 1960s and, in terms of the structure of landownership, the composition of the rural labour force, and consumer expenditure of rural households, the pattern of inequality seems to have deteriorated further in recent years.

There is also growing income inequality in the three major sectors of the economy—agriculture, unorganized non-agriculture, and organized non-agriculture. Between 1970–71 and 1980–81, the disparity ratio between the three has widened from 1.0: 1.8: 4.1 respectively, to 1.0: 2.8: 5.7 respectively (Dandekar, 1987, quoted in Dantwala, 1987).

The foregoing examples of economic analysis of social inequalities show that economists are primarily concerned with showing whether poverty is increasing or decreasing, or whether economic inequalities are more or less marked over given points of time. But such studies cannot reveal whether it is the same or different sets of people who are found in a given economic category at different points of time. For, given the same pattern of inequalities, one society may be more mobile than another. Yet, the measurement of mobility is an important indicator of social development. Therefore, for a study of social transformation for development insofar as the division of labour in society is concerned, one has to go beyond economic analysis and capture change in all the major aspects of social inequality, such as, differentiation, hierarchy and perpetuation. And one of the variables pertaining to the division of labour which can help us understand social inequalities in all its complexity is occupational prestige.

In certain respects, the variable of occupational prestige is more suitable than income for the study of social inequalities, and even more so for the study of social transformation. The pursuit of occupation is a publicly engaged activity and information about a person's occupation can be easily and accurately obtained. Not only is there a high degree of consensus among different sections of the population in giving different occupations different degrees of prestige, but occupational prestige is relatively stable at different points of time in the same society (Hodge, Siegel and Ross, 1964) as well as comparable in different societies (Inkeles and Rossi, 1956; Hodge, Treiman and Rossi, 1965).

As occupational prestige intersects with economic structure, this variable is also ideal for the study of economic development and social transformation. In this context, one of the important indicators of social transformation is intergenerational occupational mobility. Thus, social transformation leading to development is related to both the degree and pattern of occupational mobility. The development process should provide one equal opportunities to choose one's occupation irrespective of the position of one's parents or hereditary group.

Insofar as industrialism stands for a radically different kind of economy and a new occupational structure, compared with the pre-industrial economy, it definitely gives scope to a large proportion of the workers in a society to change their occupation, especially when the economy is undergoing change. This would represent a change in the degree of mobility.

One would normally expect that a change in the degree of mobility would also bring about a change in the pattern of social stratification so that in achieving new occupations the members of the society would succeed in breaking away from the rigidity of the past. But occupational mobility as such need not necessarily lead to this. For, in social transformation, it is not merely a difference in the occupation or in occupational prestige which is important but also a change in the relative occupational prestige of individuals and groups. For example, if every person in a society changed his occupation, and in doing so everyone had risen, say, one unit of occupational prestige, then the relative occupational prestige of members would have remained the same without bringing about any change in the structure of the society. It would be as if everyone were standing on their toes; in that event, whereas everyone would gain in height, the relative heights of different individuals would remain the same. For real social transformation to take place, social mobility should be random and for real social development the persons in underprivileged groupings should have better chances.

Society in India has been passing through rapid social changes, especially during the recent decades. Not only has it been exposed to global forces of change (such as, industrialization, urbanization and advancement in education) but it has also been subjected to planned development which has accelerated the tempo of change even further. Changes, which took centuries in the past to be manifested, are now telescoped into decades.

These changes have, no doubt, brought about a greater degree of differentiation in the division of labour, which is reflected in changes in the system of social stratification. Social stratification in traditional Indian society is characterized by the caste system. Simply stated, the caste system consists of a number of hereditary and normally intermarrying groups termed castes (*jatis*) living together but not socially intimate with one another in the local and regional societies. Each caste is socio-economically homogeneous, and the different castes, being at different socio-economic levels, form a status hierarchy. The status hierarchy is correlated with a ritual hierarchy which is based on the religious notions of purity and pollution.

In the past, the caste system was buttressed by the economic, political and cultural systems. The informal economic organization based mainly on agriculture, in which the household was the unit of production, resulted in the intergenerational perpetuation of inequalities and status, which is an important feature of the caste system. The monarchical and feudal systems of political power, with their characteristic legal and customary provisions, supported the hegemony of the dominant castes, which enforced the unity of the caste system. So also the dominant religio-philosophical value systems of *karma* and *dharma* sacralized the inegalitarian roots of the caste system.

India's contact with the West, with its markedly different cultural system, led to the spread of modern education, industrialization and urbanization. The country's freedom struggle and the adoption of a new political Constitution, which were inspired by the ideology of the Enlightenment, have dismantled the formal supports of the caste system and undermined its value base. (One cannot, however, gloss over the intolerable consequences of foreign rule and the studied tolerance of Indian traditions by the foreign rulers.) The logic of industrialism, which gives rise to a new occupational structure with opportunities for social and spatial mobility, leads to a disruption of homogeneity and hierarchy which are basic to the caste system. Viewed from this perspective, the changed situation in India, especially after independence, provides an ideal setting for a radical transformation of the social structure away from the caste system. The actual changes that have taken place, however, belie one's expectations.

Caste and Social Mobility: Empirical Evidence

Systematic studies on social change before independence are few and far between. But, in a skilful analysis of the economic and political changes that had taken place in Bisipara village, Orissa over a century, Bailey (1958) came to the conclusion that despite far-reaching changes in its economic and political structure, the form of social stratification in the village, based on the caste system, had remained virtually unimpaired. Although the relative positions of some of the castes in the caste hierarchy had changed, the caste system as such had not broken down. Even though some castes had benefited more than others, the ability of those castes to derive differential benefits from the changes were themselves related to the very caste system. By and large, the economic and political changes had been channelled through the existing social structure.

Although confined to a single village, Bailey's study almost sums up the situation in the country as a whole before independence, which was one of change and continuity, and all the data point to the resilience of the structure of the Indian society. The situation has not changed much after independence, despite the heightened tempo of change. Even the fact of planned development does not appear to have made much difference in this respect, which is not surprising. For, although the transformation of the social structure from its restrictive, non-egalitarian and socially exclusive form into one of freedom and equality of opportunity and social inclusivism, has been one of the major objectives of Indian planning, the attention so far has been mainly on economic development, without making any direct attempts at changing the social structure. Consequently, most of the economic changes that have taken place have been absorbed by the social structure to subserve its existing pattern.

Again, there is no systematic evidence covering the whole country regarding intergenerational occupational mobility to corroborate the above statements about social change in India at present. One of the major hurdles in undertaking such studies is the lack of a standardized scale or index of occupational prestige. Therefore, scholars have been left to their own devices to gather whatever evidence they can. It is such evidence, pieced together, which will now be presented to indicate the prevailing trends in social mobility and social transformation.

One of the earliest studies on intergenerational occupational mobility in India was conducted by Sovani and his associates in Poona in 1954 (Sovani *et al.*, 1956). However, the prestige gradation of occupations in this study was done in an arbitrary fashion. One of the major flaws in this technique was the classification of all the agricultural occupations (including those of owner-cultivators) in the category of unskilled manual work, representing the lowest grade of occupations. This has resulted in a great degree of bias in the analysis, as a very high proportion of the fathers and grandfathers of the subjects studied were cultivators with varying sizes of landholdings. As a consequence of this bias, the study shows a relatively low degree of mobility between the grandfathers and the fathers of the subjects and relatively high degree of mobility between the fathers of the subjects and the subjects themselves. Intergenerational mobility was relatively higher among the migrants than among those born in the city due largely to the fact that the former came mostly from villages where their fathers were generally cultivators, so that any occupation of the subjects in the city, which was above the lowest gradation, meant upward intergenerational occupational mobility. All the same, the study of intergenerational occupational mobility in Poona revealed a relatively high degree of stability, indicating a strong influence of the status of the parents on the status attainment of their sons. However, the Poona study covers the situation prior to the impact of planned social change.

The study on the intergenerational occupational mobility of the rural population of Punjab (Sharda, 1977) is more relevant. The

author has analysed the occupational data from the village studies
conducted by the Census Department, Government of India, in
1962–63. A set of eleven villages was purposively chosen from
among the available studies. An occupational prestige scale was
devised by the author by piecing together information from several
studies on occupational prestige grading already conducted in
different parts of the country, including Punjab. Although this
scale suffers from many limitations, it has the merit of employing
objective procedures. Moreover, the scale was specially adapted
to gauge the prestige of rural occupations. Sharda found that the
coefficient of correlation between the occupational prestige of the
subjects and their fathers was of the order of 0.673. This shows a
high degree of stability in the social stratification of rural Punjab.
How strong is the influence of occupational prestige of parents on
that of their sons in Punjab can be inferred further from the fact
that the corresponding coefficient of correlation for the rural
population of the United States was only 0.120.

Punjab (including its neighbouring state Haryana) is perhaps the
most important region in India for the study of social change and
social mobility as it has been the most influenced by economic
development, being the precursor of the Green Revolution in
India. A study of intergenerational occupational mobility
conducted in 1980 in three villages of Punjab and Haryana
(D'Souza, 1985) takes into account the impact of the Green
Revolution on social change (Sharda's study of rural Punjab,
considered above, refers to a point in time, 1962–63, which was
prior to the onset of the Green Revolution, with 1966 as its
watershed). The three villages—Ugala in Haryana, and Ghagga
and Ghudani Kalan in Punjab—were large with populations of
4,800, 5,143 and 4,380, respectively. They also had a substantial
proportion of non-agricultural occupations, ranging from 29 to 35
per cent, with the resulting diversification of the economy and
differentiation of the occupational structure.

Based on a random sample of 33 per cent of the households in
each village, the study was conducted in a systematic manner
insofar as the occupational prestige and caste rankings were concerned. Both the occupations and the castes were ranked by the
villagers themselves. The study confirmed the assumption that the
hierarchy of caste status is related to the occupational prestige of
members of different castes; the product moment coefficients of

correlation between the status of the castes and the average occupational prestige score of their members were 0.715, 0.627 and 0.724 in Ugala (15 castes), Ghagga (16 castes) and Ghudani Kalan (12 castes), respectively.

Since the changes in the economy were recent ones, it was assumed that the sons of the heads of the households would have had the opportunity of shifting from the traditional occupations of their fathers and, if so, it would bring about changes in the existing caste structure. But a comparison of the occupational prestige of the heads of the households and those of their sons gave the product moment coefficients of correlation of 0.862, 0.787 and 0.852 in Ugala, Ghagga and Ghudani Kalan, respectively, all of which were greater than what Sharda found for his rural sample at an earlier point of time. Accordingly, a comparison of castes in terms of the average occupational prestige of the fathers, on the one hand, and that of the sons, on the other, gave rank difference coefficients of correlations of 0.927, 0.908 and 0.956 in Ugala, Ghagga and Ghudani Kalan, respectively. These findings would lead one to the conclusion that economic changes until then had not resulted in much social mobility and hence had hardly affected the social structure.

A major question that arises from the above facts is why, despite far-reaching changes in economic activities, the degree of occupational mobility was so low? An analysis of the economic activities and their utilization shows that there were a variety of new economic opportunities which had been utilized by the villagers. But the pattern of utilization seems to have been influenced by the caste structure, which accounts for the low degree of intergenerational occupational mobility.

At least four different categories of new economic opportunities were noticeable in the villages. These included occupations in trade followed by 6 to 12 per cent of the workers in different villages; jobs in the government and industrial organisations in the village representing the formal sector, which were filled by 8 to 9 per cent of the workers in the different villages; jobs outside the village held by commuting workers who comprised 4 to 14 per cent; and urban occupations which were availed of by 10 to 29 per cent of the sons of heads of households in different villages who had migrated. The volume of new opportunities was quite substantial in the aggregate.

The advantage derived from the new opportunities depends not only upon the proportion of workers who have grasped them, but also upon the prestige levels of the new jobs. For example, an agricultural worker taking up the job of an unskilled worker in a factory is not likely to gain much, by our reckoning. In Table 2.1, the scores on a summary index of the new economic opportunities accruing to the members of the different castes in the three different villages is presented. The index scores take into account the percentage of members of a caste who have gained the new occupations as well as the prestige levels of such occupations.

Table 2.1
Index of Utilization of Opportunities in a Changing Economy

Ugala		Ghagga		Ghudani Kalan	
Caste	*Index Score*	*Caste*	*Index Score*	*Caste*	*Index Score*
Higher Castes					
Brahmin	8.50	Brahmin	3.51	Brahmin	19.52
Rajput	4.30	Bania	15.79	Jat	4.81
Bania	15.38	Khatri	20.57		
Khatri	9.17	Jat	0.51		
Intermediate Castes					
Kamboj	1.28	Tarkhan	2.41		
Dhobi/Kahar	1.19				
Lower Castes					
Bazigar	0.52	Bazigar	0.74	Ramdasia	5.37
Ramdasia	3.16	Ramdasia	0.90		
*Miscellaneous**	7.34		1.40		5.72
Total Sample	5.74		3.08		6.34

Note: * Miscellaneous includes all castes with less than 10 sample households in a caste.
Source: D'Souza, 1985.

As can be seen from the table, the broad pattern of utilization of the new opportunities is the same in all the three villages. First, the higher castes have availed themselves of the new opportunities to a greater degree than the lower ones. Second, among the higher castes, the cultivating castes of Rajputs in Ugala and Jats in

Ghagga and Ghudani Kalan have benefited the least in their respective villages; the owner-cultivators are usually tied to their land and are, therefore, less able to grasp the new opportunities. Third, the trading castes of Bania in Ugala and Bania and Khatri in Ghagga have benefited the most from the growth of trade in these villages. On the other hand, in Ghudani Kalan, which is noted for the development of the organized sector such as government employment, it is the professional caste of Brahmins which has benefited the most.

The fact that opportunities in the new economy have accrued to persons according to their position in the social structure explains why despite changes in the economy, the caste hierarchies in the villages have been maintained. The persistence of caste hierarchies, however, is not without modification. For example, unlike the traditional pattern whereby the trading castes of Bania and Khatri in a Punjab village are usually ranked lower than the dominant cultivating caste of Jat, in Ghagga the positions have been reversed. This has been rendered possible by the excessive growth of trade opportunities.

The channelling of the new economic opportunities through the existing structure also brings about some overall changes in the social structure when the economy changes. For instance, when trade grows in a region as a result of agricultural development, as in the Punjab, apart from the towns, some of the villages also grow and become trade towns. But it is usually villages with relatively larger populations of trading castes which tend to draw trading activities into the village and, when trade gains momentum, they tend to draw more members of the trading castes from the surrounding areas. In this manner, the trading castes would be over-represented in a trading village or trade town. This process is clearly demonstrated in Rayya, which is in Amritsar district of Punjab, which shot into the category of trade town in 1981 with 60 per cent of its workforce in trade and with a 55 per cent increase in its population during 1971–81 (Sethi, 1982).

The spurt of trade in Rayya had naturally drawn a greater proportion of the population of the trading castes into the town; whereas these castes (such as, Khatri, Arora and Bania) constituted only 13 per cent among the original residents, they constituted 46 per cent of the immigrants. The growing opportunities in trade had given full scope for economic adjustment for the members of the trading castes among whom virtually all the heads of households were occupied in trade. But the bourgeoning activity in trade had drawn into its fold members of other castes also, as the trading castes could not exhaust all the new openings.

However, the new entrants to trade from the other castes had adopted such lines of trade which had some connection with their traditional caste occupation. Thus, the Jats (cultivating caste) had set up wholesale trade in foodgrains or servicing facilities for tractors, persons of the carpenter caste had opened timber depots or furniture shops, those with tailoring as their traditional occupation had started cloth shops, those who were traditionally domestic servants had opened small eating places, and those who had earlier prepared eathernware utensils were now selling aluminium and stainless steel untensils. Another significant feature about the new entrants to trade was that members of the higher castes had invested a larger amount of capital in business and trade than members of the lower castes, thereby contributing to the stability of the caste hierarchy.

Because of the phenomenal change in the occupational structure of Rayya, there had been a considerable degree of occupational mobility. But, despite such vast changes, the average occupational prestige of the different castes had remained more or less constant in relative terms. This is because, in shifting to new occupations, the members of the higher castes had succeeded in securing occupations of higher prestige and those of the lower castes could obtain only occupations of lower prestige; thus, when the average occupational prestige of various castes is compared according to different pairs of significant variables, we get the following high degrees of coefficients of correlation:

Pairs of Variables	*Coefficients of Correlation*
Original residents and immigrants	0.818
Respondents' grandfathers and fathers	0.921
Respondents and their fathers	0.932
Respondents and their sons	0.819

In other words, the immigrants belonging to a given caste had secured occupations consistent with the occupational prestige of the members of the same caste who were the original residents of the town. So also the relative positions of the castes in terms of their average occupational prestige had changed very little, if at all, over four generations. What had greatly changed was the population composition of the various castes, with the population of the trading castes increasing very markedly.

The study referred to above proposes that economic-functional differences among villages or towns are related to the differences in their caste composition. The existence of such a relationship is further supported by a comparative study of two small towns (class V category)—one trading and the other industrial—in Jalandhar district, Punjab (Gill, 1983). It has already been indicated that where the predominant function of a town is trade, the population of the trading castes is over-represented in that town. On the other hand, the growth of small and medium scale industries (for which Punjab is noted) is spearheaded by the caste of Ramgarhias (traditional carpenters and blacksmiths). Therefore, the newly emerging industrial towns in the Punjab are over-represented by the Ramgarhia caste.

Table 2.2 profiles the caste composition of Goraya (an industrial town) and Nurmahal (a trade town) in terms of their caste ranking, percentage of population and average occupational prestige. Only the castes common to both the towns are mentioned and the rest of the population is classified under the category 'Miscellaneous'. Both Goraya and Nurmahal are small towns, with a population of 7,077 and 7,329, respectively, in 1979. However, whereas Nurmahal had been a town for a longer period, Goraya was declared as a town only in the 1971 Census.

Attention may be focused on two major aspects of information in Table 2.2, namely, the population of the major castes which is directly linked with the dominant functions of the towns, and the relative status positions of some of the castes. Since the Ramgarhias took the initiative in starting industry in Goraya, they constitute 18.26 per cent of the population, as against a mere 3.83 per cent in Nurmahal, the trade town. On the other hand, in Nurmahal, the trading castes of Khatri and Arora constitute 27.97 per cent of the population of the town as against 16.03 in Goraya. It should be borne in mind that the industrial town also generates a substantial amount of trading activity and, accordingly, the trading castes in Goraya also consitute a sizeable percentage of the population.

Table 2.2

Caste Profile of an Industrial Town and a Trade Town in Terms of Ranks, Population Percentage and Average Occupational Prestige

Caste Rank	Goraya			Nurmahal		
	Caste	Population (Percentage)	Average Occupational Prestige	Caste	Population (Percentage)	Average Occupational Prestige
1	Jat	11.87	5.00	Brahmin	12.58	4.33
2	Ramgarhia	18.26	4.76	Jat	5.25	5.27
3	Brahmin	12.39	4.36	Khatri	17.97	5.03
4	Khatri	5.64	5.38	Arora	10.00	4.72
5	Arora	10.39	4.80	Suniar	2.58	5.00
6	Suniar	1.20	5.00	Ramgarhia	3.83	3.50
7	Jhewar	4.85	2.33	Chhimba	2.37	4.00
8	Chhimba	4.61	3.71	Jhewar	4.56	4.10
9	Nai	1.74	3.33	Nai	2.81	2.00
10	Ad-Dharmi	17.41	2.08	Ad-Dharmi	24.26	1.73
11	Balmiki	3.65	1.00	Balmiki	2.96	1.00
	Miscellaneous	7.99	—	Miscellaneous	11.01	—
	Total	100	3.99		100	3.79

Source: Gill, 1983.
Note: Goraya represents an industrial town and Nurmahal a trade town.

As regards the relative status positions, the most important fact to be noted is the relatively high rank of the Ramgarhias in Goraya. Here, they were ranked even higher than the Brahmins and the trading castes. In general, the Ramgarhias are included among the Backward Classes and, in fact, they were ranked as such in Nurmahal where their occupational prestige was correspondingly low. In Goraya, the Ramgarhias not only constituted the single largest caste but they also owned the largest number of industrial establishments. Their dominance in the town was also indicated by the fact that the chairman of the Goraya Municipal Committee was a Ramgarhia.

It may be noted that the traditional dominant caste of Jats in Goraya was still held in the highest esteem, despite the fact that the dominance of agriculture in this small town has yielded place to industry. However, the Jats have been able to maintain their pre-eminence by taking advantage of industry and some of the other top urban occupations besides being the largest group of owner-cultivators. On the other hand, the trading castes have not reached the apex of the caste hierarchy in Nurmahal in spite of the fact they held a pre-eminent position in trade in this trade town. The most prestigious caste in Nurmahal were the Brahmins while the Jats and the trading castes were grouped together next in importance. Here, also, the pre-eminent position of the Brahmins was due to their diversification and their holding some top occupations in agriculture and trade and middle level positions in formal organizations. The chairman of the Municipal Committee of Nurmahal was a Brahmin. Nevertheless, the link between caste and economic function is very much in evidence in both the towns.

Social Mobility: The Religious and Regional Factors

At the primary level of analysis it can be seen that the changes in the economy are channelled through the caste system. Therefore, rural-urban migration, which is based on economic development, is also channelled through the caste system. Thus it has been pointed out that among the higher castes in the Punjab, the cultivating caste of Jats is least prone to migrate to the urban areas. But, on the other hand, the professional caste of Brahmins and the trading castes of Khatris, Aroras and Banias and the carpenter caste of Ramgarhias have shown a great propensity to move to the urban areas. We have so far not focused on the Scheduled Castes who form more than one quarter of the population of the Punjab. It is sufficient to point out that among them one of the larger segments known as the Mazhabis are more integrated into the rural economy as agricultural labourers and hence are relatively less mobile. On the other hand, Scheduled Castes, such as, the Chamars, Ad-Dharmis and Balmikis, following occupations such as leather work, crafts and scavenging service, respectively, are more free to migrate to the urban areas.

However, at the secondary level of analysis of social change, the category of religion appears to be a significant variable. This is because, often, the caste composition of the different religious categories in a region tends to be different, which is clearly the case in the Punjab. In Punjab every one of the major castes differentially affected by economic change belongs almost exclusively either to the Hindu or the Sikh religion. The Jats, Ramgarhias and Mazhabis are almost exclusively Sikhs. Among the trading castes of Khatris and Aroras, a small fraction, say about 10 to 15 per cent, are Sikhs. Besides the overwhelming majority of the Khatris and the Aroras, all the Brahmins and the Banias and the Scheduled Castes of Chamars, Ad-Dharmis and Balmikis belong to the Hindu religion. This illustration is not exhaustive but represents the general situation.

However, most of the Sikhs belonging to the Jat and Mazhabi castes who follow agricultural occupations are less prone to migrate to the urban areas. The notable exceptions are the Ramgarhias and the Khatri and Arora Sikhs. On the other hand, almost all the Hindu castes follow mostly non-agricultural occupations in the rural areas and, being footloose, are more prone to migrate to the urban areas. Thus, the Hindu and Sikh castes are differently affected by economic change and hence show diametrically opposite trends as regards rural-urban migration. The caste polarization in the migration pattern, therefore, results in a religious polarization. The Sikhs tend to be concentrated in the rural areas and the Hindus in the urban areas.

On the basis of the way in which economic change is channelled through the social structure and the resulting pattern of rural-urban migration, the following generalizations may be drawn. In a typical Punjab village, because of the preponderance of Jats and Mazhabis, the majority of the population is Sikh. When the village becomes a trade town, as in the case of Rayya referred to above, the Hindu population increases, as the migrant trading castes belong mainly to the Hindu religion. In Rayya, among the original residents who represented the pre-urban situation, the Sikhs comprised 61 per cent of the population whereas among the inmigrants their percentage was only 43. At the time of the study, the Hindus had already become the majority comprising 51 per cent of the total population. Any further growth of the town would be bound to result in an increase in the Hindu majority. The growth of the Hindu majority of a town would be slower in an industrial town than in a trade town, as an industrial town attracts a greater proportion of Ramgarhias who are mostly Sikhs. For example, between Goraya and Nurmahal (which were of the same size and are located in the same district), the Hindu population in the former, which was an industrial town, was 63 per cent whereas in the latter, which was a trade town, it was 81 per cent.

What is happening at the micro-level of the village and small town is being reflected at the macro-level in larger regions and the state as a whole. In a study of the migration pattern in Ludhiana and its hinterland (conducted by the Demographic Research Centre, Panjab University, 1983, as yet unpublished), it was found that whereas the percentage distribution of the Sikh and Hindu population in the rural areas was 73.81 and 25.68, respectively, in the urban areas it was 28.87 and 71.13, respectively, which was almost of the reverse order (see Table 2.3). The migration patterns too were of a similar order; whereas the immigrants in the rural areas were 73.91 per cent Sikh and 26.09 per cent Hindu, those in the urban areas 28.88 per cent Sikh and 69.59 per cent Hindu.

Since the rural population represents a reservoir from which the urban migrants are drawn and since the rural population is largely Sikh, most of the urban immigrants should have been Sikh. But the contrary occurred because of the caste-selective basis of migration which favours the Hindus. In fact, the Hindu trading caste of Khatris alone accounted for 36 per cent of the total migrants whereas the corresponding percentage of the Sikh cultivating caste of Jats was only 5 per cent (not shown in the table).

The processes of economic change, social mobility and migration,

Table 2.3

Migration Pattern in Rural and Urban Ludhiana According to Religion (1983)

Religion	Rural Areas				Urban Areas			
	Original Residents		Immigrants		Original Residents		Immigrants	
	Number	Percentage	Number	Percentage	Number	Percentage	Number	Percentage
Sikh	434	73.81	51	73.91	41	28.87	283	28.88
Hindu	151	25.68	18	26.09	101	71.13	682	69.59
Muslim	3	00.51	—	—	—	—	12	1.22
Christian	—	—	—	—	—	—	3	0.31
Total	588	100	69	100	142	100	980	100

Source: Demographic Research Centre, Panjab University, 1983. 'Migration and Fertility,' unpublished.

which are channelled through the social structure, account for the high degree of polarization between the Hindus and Sikhs in the rural and urban areas. According to the 1981 Census, whereas the Hindus and Sikhs formed 37 and 61 per cent of the total population, their distribution in the rural population was 25 and 71 per cent, respectively, as against their distribution of 64 and 33 per cent, respectively, in the urban areas. By analysing the differential representation of the Hindus and Sikhs according to their economic-functional character as well as the size of the towns and cities in Punjab, I have showed elsewhere (D'Souza, 1982) that the rural-urban polarization of Hindus and Sikhs at the macro-level is, in fact, a result of changes taking place at the micro-levels.

To recapitulate the broad trends of social change in the Punjab, first, economic development has been generally channelled through the existing social structure. Since the higher castes have benefited more than the lower ones, even when all the castes have benefited from change, the socio-economic homogeneity of castes and their status hierarchy have not been affected much. However, there are exceptional cases where some castes have benefited more than what was warranted by their position in the caste hierarchy, by virtue of the fact that their traditional occupation gave them an edge over the others in gaining from the new economy. Such changes have not upset the caste system but have been adjusted to in the social structure by bringing about appropriate changes in the relative positions of the castes in the status hierarchy.

Economic development has accelerated the growth of urbanization which provides better economic opportunities. The growth of urbanization, however, is spearheaded by certain castes, especially those belonging to the upper levels of the caste hierarchy, which are therefore over-represented in the urban areas. However, among the higher castes, the cultivating castes which dominate the rural scene are least represented in the urban areas. Therefore, there is a polarization not only in the general composition of the rural and urban population but also in the elite sections of the two areas.

The caste system is the primary social structural factor through which mobility is channelled. But insofar as different castes are differentially distributed in the major religious groupings in

Punjab, the rural-urban polarization of the caste structure is also reflected in the rural-urban polarization of the religious categories.

There is reason to believe that what has been happening in the Punjab has parallels in other parts of the country as well. The general aspects of these changes are related to the caste system which, except for a few areas of tribal dominance, is ubiquitous in India. There is evidence to show that, as in the Punjab, in every region of India the higher castes are over-represented in the urban areas; however, the castes comprising the Backward Classes and Scheduled Castes, especially the latter, are greatly under-represented. Again, as in the Punjab, in every region the dominant landowning and cultivating castes are under-represented in the urban areas.

It is also true that the caste composition of the various groupings in the social structure of a given region is different. What is variable in this case is the salience or the importance of the type of structural groupings which may vary from region to region. For example, the salient macro-structural groupings in the Punjab are the Hindu and the Sikh religious categories. But in the neighbouring state of Haryana, which has an overwhelming Hindu majority, the social-structural groupings are the Haryanvi cultivating castes which are dominant in the rural areas and the Punjabi trading castes which are dominant in the urban areas. The antagonistic parties in this case are the territorial groupings. The pattern in Haryana is repeated in more regions than the Punjab pattern, although the latter seems to attract greater attention. The conflict of economic and political interests of religious groupings leads to so-called communal demands and those of territorial groups leads to nativistic demands. But, basically, both kinds of demands stem from the same general conditions, namely, the channelling of economic change through the caste system.

In Punjab, the minority religious grouping (namely, the Hindus) is over-represented in the urban areas. But it is significant to note that the minority religious groupings are over-represented in the urban areas in almost every region and every state as well as in the country. Here the terms minority and majority are defined in relation to the geographical or administrative territory under reference (D'Souza, 1983). The reasons for such a consistent trend also seem to be the same almost everywhere. Generally, it is found that in a given region the major landowning and cultivating castes belong to the majority religious category and the members of minority groupings follow footloose occupations which push them to the urban areas.

All these comparable general trends noticeable in different parts of the country indicate that more or less similar changes are operating at the micro-level everywhere. Invariably, such trends are contrary to the emergence of a just social order.

3

Impact of Social Hierarchy and Regional Disparities on the Development of Social Groups

In a broad sense, industrialism released certain forces which may be considered to have had a positive effect on the development of the individual. One of the consequences of industrialization which has had a tremendous impact on the development of the individual is the change in the structure and function of the family. In pre-industrial society, the family was both a unit of production and consumption. But industrialization, because of its formal organization of economic activities, has deprived the family of its production function besides modifying its function of consumption.

When the family also served as the unit of production, a person's occupation and status depended upon the socio-economic conditions of the family which rarely underwent change. Therefore, in pre-industrial societies, it is difficult for an individual to alter his life-chances, and there is a strong tendency for the intergenerational perpetuation of inherited inequalities. In other words, in pre-industrial societies the individual is denied the opportunities of development. On the other hand, the new economic organization of industrialism gave an opportunity to individuals to acquire new skills and occupations with the possibility of changing their inherited life-chances.

Thus, for the first time, a relationship between education and occupational prestige was brought about, on a larger scale, through industrialization. In the pre-industrial, agricultural societies such a relationship hardly existed. Further, a relationship between education and occupational prestige is found to a high degree in the urban areas in which the formal organizations are usually concentrated. Hence, in all industrializing societies, we have, at the macro-level, the often observed relationships among the variables of education, proportion of occupations in industy and urbanization, which are regarded as proxies for the characteristics of modernization. In this analysis, we shall call these demographic features the variables of modernization.

Because of its potential for bringing about far-reaching changes in society, many social scientists seem to have espoused the capacity of the process of modernization to bring about a wholesome transformation of society in a desired direction. In doing so, however, they do not seem to have reckoned with the resilience of some of the structural dimensions in society which have the power to channel change in directions unanticipated by the enthusiasts of modernization. We have already seen in the preceding chapter how opportunities in the new economy accrue to people according to their position in the social structure.

Another aspect of the social structure is the regional dimension so that people living in different regions tend to have different degrees of opportunities in the new economy. This is common knowledge, but the systematic features of the regional dimension will be shown presently. This chapter shows how among other factors, the position of a social group in the social hierarchy as well as its residence in a given region affect its chances of benefiting from industrialization and economic development.

Economic Development and Modernization: Regional Disparities

First, let us discuss briefly the nature of the regional disparities in the variables of modernization and their response to economic development. Because of the constraints of using available data from the census publications, the percentage of literacy (also referred to as the literacy rate), the percentage of the urban population and the percentage of non-agricultural workers may be regarded as variables of modernization for this study. The variable of economic development is a complex one and can be expressed in several different indices. However, since this is not a study of economic development *per se*, our purpose will be served by choosing just one index of this variable, that is the per capita domestic product, which is widely used by economists.

A comparative picture of economic development and moderni-zation in the various states of India for 1971 and 1981 is provided in Tables 3.1–3.3. Only the larger states of India are considered; Assam, where the census was not taken in 1981, is excluded. In Table 3.3, the percentages in Tables 3.1 and 3.2 are expressed as relative ranks. The state-wise distribution of the different variables shows certain patterns which have remained, by and large, the same in 1971 and 1981.

Table 3.1
State-wise Indices of Modernization and Development, 1971 (Percentage)

State	Literacy	Urban Population	Non-Agri-cultural Workers	Per Capita Domestic Product (Rs at Current Prices)
Andhra Pradesh	24.57	19.31	29.90	586
Bihar	19.94	9.99	17.74	418
Gujarat	35.79	28.07	34.40	845
Haryana	26.89	17.66	34.71	932
Karnataka	31.52	24.30	33.29	675
Kerala	60.42	16.24	51.51	636
Madhya Pradesh	22.14	16.28	20.58	489
Maharashtra	39.18	31.16	35.13	811
Orissa	26.18	8.41	22.56	541
Punjab	33.67	23.73	37.33	1,067
Rajasthan	19.07	17.63	25.77	629
Tamil Nadu	39.46	30.25	38.28	616
Uttar Pradesh	21.70	14.02	22.62	493
West Bengal	33.20	24.75	41.58	729
India	29.45	19.31	30.28	638

Source: *Census of India*, 1971, Union Primary Census Abstract; Chakravarty (1987: 127).

The most important feature of the distribution of data is that there is a wide variation in the distribution of every variable (Tables 3.1 and 3.2) in the different states—the range of variation being larger in 1981 than in 1971. Thus the percentage of literacy varied from 19.07 in Rajasthan to 60.42 in Kerala, and from 24.38 in Rajasthan to 70.42 in Kerala in 1971 and 1981 respectively, the

Table 3.2
State-wise Indices of Modernization and Development, 1981 (Percentage)

State	Literacy	Urban Population	Non-Agri- cultural Workers	Per Capita Domestic Product (Rs at Current Prices)
Andhra Pradesh	29.94	23.32	30.47	1,360
Bihar	26.20	12.47	20.93	958
Gujarat	43.70	31.10	29.88	2,150
Haryana	36.14	21.86	39.23	2,447
Karnataka	38.46	28.89	34.97	1,559
Kerala	70.42	18.74	58.70	1,540
Madhya Pradesh	27.87	20.29	23.80	1,237
Maharashtra	47.18	35.03	38.25	2,329
Orissa	34.23	11.79	25.30	1,286
Punjab	40.86	27.68	41.97	2,842
Rajasthan	24.38	20.98	31.09	1,220
Tamil Nadu	46.76	32.95	39.09	1,413
Uttar Pradesh	27.16	17.95	25.50	1,212
West Bengal	40.94	26.47	44.71	1,586
India	36.23	23.70	33.48	1,559

Source: *Census of India*, 1981, Primary Census Abstract, General Population; Chakravarty (1987: 127).

range having widened from 41.35 to 46.04 between the two points of time. Similarly, between 1971 and 1981, the range of variation in distribution has widened from 22.75 to 23.24 in the case of the percentage of the urban population, from 33.77 to 37.77 in the case of the percentage of non-agricultural workers, and from 649 to 1,884 in the case of the per capita domestic product (PCDP). In other words, with growth, the difference between the most developed and the least developed states in a given variable has widened.

Another way of looking at the disparities is to compare the ratio between the states with the highest and the lowest distribution of a variable at two points of time. The ratios for the different variables from 1961 to 1981 are given below.

The ratios in all the cases are very high. In the case of the indices of modernization (namely, literacy, urbanization and non-agricultural workers), the ratios are more or less of a similar order and they have all tended to decline from 1971 to 1981.

Variable	Ratio Between States with the Highest and Lowest Distribution		
	1961*	1971	1981
Percentage of literacy	3.08	3.17	2.90
Percentage of urban population	4.46	3.70	2.97
Percentage of non-agricultural workers	2.98	3.13	2.80
Per capita domestic product	2.52	2.55	2.96

* Not shown in table.

However, in the case of PCDP, although the ratio was relatively smaller in 1961, unlike the trends in the other variables, it has increased in 1981. It would thus appear that the economic disparity between the most developed and the least developed states has widened far more than the disparities in the other variables.

A second important feature of the distributions as presented in Table 3.3 is that the relative positions or ranks of the various states

Table 3.3

State-wise Ranks on Indices of Modernization and Development, 1971 and 1981

State	Literacy		Urban Population		Non-agri-cultural Workers		Per Capita Domestic Product	
	1971	1981	1971	1981	1971	1981	1971	1981
Andhra Pradesh	10	10	7	7	9	10	10	9
Bihar	13	13	13	13	14	14	14	14
Gujarat	4	4	3	3	7	4	3	4
Haryana	8	8	8	8	6	5	2	2
Karnataka	7	7	5	4	8	8	6	6
Kerala	1	1	11	11	1	1	7•	7
Madhya Pradesh	11	11	10	10	13	13	13	11
Maharashtra	3	2	1	1	5	7	4	3
Orissa	9	9	14	14	12	12	11	10
Punjab	5	6	6	5	4	3	1	1
Rajasthan	14	14	9	9	10	9	8	12
Tamil Nadu	2	3	2	2	3	6	9	8
Uttar Pradesh	12	12	12	12	11	11	12	13
West Bengal	6	5	4	6	2	2	5	5

Source: Tables 3.1 and 3.2.

on any of the variables have remained almost the same in 1971 and 1981. The coefficients of correlations of the ranks of the states on the different variables at the two points of time are uniformly very high, as follows:

Variable	Coefficient of Correlation
Percentage of literacy in 1971 and 1981	0.991
Percentage of the urban population in 1971 and 1981	0.987
Percentage of non-agricultural workers in 1971 and 1981	0.943
Per capita domestic product in 1971 and 1981	0.943

Thus, whereas the inequalities have tended to widen over the years the relative positions of the states have tended to remain constant.

A third feature which emerges from an examination of the data presented in Tables 3.1, 3.2 and 3.3 is that with certain exceptions, the ranks of the various states on the different variables are on the whole consistent with one another, which is especially true in the case of the variables of modernization. Among the exceptions, the most discrepant case is that of Kerala. Although it ranks first among the states in literacy and non-agricultural workers, it comes very near the bottom in urbanization. One major reason for this marked discrepancy is Kerala's peculiar topographical situation resulting in a dispersed residential pattern which is uncommon in the rest of India. As a result of this unusual situation, the usual definition of urbanization is inadequate to capture the urban character of Kerala. The pre-eminent position of Kerala in education and non-agricultural workers is also inconsistent with its rather low standing in the PCDP. Again, this can be explained by the fact that the high percentage of non-agricultural workers in this state has been induced more by the rapid growth of education than by the growth of industrialization.

First a look at the inter-correlations among the variables of modernization which are given below:

Pairs of Variables	Coefficients of Correlation		
	1961	1971	1981
Literacy and urbanization*	0.804	0.872	0.816
Urbanization and non-agricultural workers*	0.705	0.834	0.789
Literacy and non-agricultural workers	0.794	0.887	0.894

* Excluding Kerala

All these coefficients of correlation are very high at the three points of time—1961, 1971 and 1981.

So also, as the following figures indicate, the correlations between the per capita domestic product with each of the variables of modernization are quite high though, not as high as their inter-correlation just considered:

Variables Correlated with Per Capita Domestic Product	Coefficients of Correlation		
	1961	1971	1981
Literacy	0.559	0.591	0.741
Urbanization	0.828	0.623	0.679
Non-agricultural workers	0.637	0.705	0.771

These coefficients of correlation (with one exception) have become consistently stronger in 1981 as compared with 1961 and 1971. All the same, the relatively lower influence of the variables of modernization on the variable of economic development compared to their mutual intercorrelation can be explained by the fact that economic development of the different states is also influenced by the developmental policies of the government. For example, in the initial stages of planned development, much emphasis was laid on agricultural development, and the states which responded most to this stimulus—such as Punjab and Haryana—were not necessarily those which ranked highest on the variables of modernization. But our data also indicate that the states which have shown a spurt in economic development are also showing a tendency to advance in the variables of modernization, which is reflected in the strengthening of the coefficients of correlation from 1961 to 1981. Moreover, even though development planning has sometimes upset the relative positions of some of the states as regards economic inequalities, the inequalities themselves have widened.

On the whole it is quite clear that the variables of modernization and economic development are embedded in a matrix of interrelationships, which would account for the relatively stable pattern of inequalities observed among the different states. As will be clear presently, similar patterns of inequalities also exist between smaller regional units (such as the districts of a state) as are found between larger units (such as the states of the country).

The inequalities among regions are nothing but the inequalities of peoples living in those regions. Thus, regional disparities affect the fortunes of the people living in different regions, and hence exacerbate the inequalities existing among the hierarchical groupings.

Widening Educational Inequalities among the Scheduled Castes of Punjab

The combined effect of social hierarchy and regional disparities can be illustrated with reference to the growing educational inequalities of the Scheduled Castes in the state of Punjab. It is generally noticed that when development takes place, the inequalities which exist among the different segments of a population increase. A striking example is in the development of the Scheduled Castes (Chitnis, 1972). The reasons for this were examined elsewhere (D'Souza, 1980). The relevant findings of this study will be detailed here.

Punjab, among the larger states of the country, has the largest proportion of Scheduled Castes (about 27 per cent in 1981), although this is countervailed by the total absence of Scheduled Tribes. As in many other parts of the country, the Scheduled Castes in Punjab lag behind the general population in their education. The percentage of Scheduled Caste literates in 1961, 1971 and 1981 was 10.30, 16.12 and 23.86 respectively as compared with the corresponding percentages of 26.78, 33.39 and 40.86 respectively among the general population.

However, from the development point of view it is not the absolute educational growth alone, as indicated by percentage increase, but the growth in education of the Scheduled Castes in relation to the growth in education of the rest of the population, which is even more significant. This relative growth may be obtained through the index of educational equality (IEE) which can be worked out as follows:

$$\text{IEE} = \frac{\text{Percentage of literate among the Scheduled Castes}}{\text{Percentage of literate among the rest of the population}} \times 100$$

A coefficient of equality equal to 100 would imply that the educational level of the Scheduled Castes is equal to that of the rest of the population. Any score below 100 would mean that the Scheduled Castes are lagging behind while a higher score would signify their advancement over the rest of the population.

Using this yardstick, whereas the Scheduled Castes in Punjab still lag far behind the rest of the population, they have nevertheless made some progress over the decades, their IEE scores being 32, 40 and 51 in 1961, 1971 and 1981 respectively. But when we consider educational equality among the Scheduled Castes *inter se*, the situation reverses itself.

Although the census of 1961 and 1971 lists thirty-seven Scheduled Castes, the largest four castes among them together comprise 83 per cent. They, along with the next seven castes in order of their size, account for 94 per cent of the total population of the Scheduled Castes of the state. Some data, including the coefficient of equality of these four large and seven medium-sized castes, are given in Table 3.4. The coefficient of equality of the Scheduled Castes (SC) *inter se* is obtained as follows:

$$\text{IEE (SC \textit{inter se})} = \frac{\text{Percentage of literate in a given Scheduled Caste}}{\text{Percentage of literate among the rest of the Scheduled Castes}} \times 100$$

Table 3.4 shows that there is much variation in the educational achievement of the Scheduled Castes, the coefficients of equality

Table 3.4

Educational Achievement of the Large and Medium-sized Scheduled Caste Groups of Punjab, 1961–71

Caste	Population in 1971	1961		1971	
		% of Literate Persons	Coefficient of Equality	% of Literate Persons	Coefficient of Equality
Ad-Dharmi	4,39,632	16.01	175	27.27	189
Balmiki	4,01,962	7.76	72	13.84	84
Bauria	42,713	5.36	52	5.99	37
Bazigar	75,092	3.18	31	6.61	40
Chamar	9,81,471	12.01	125	19.83	136
Dhanak	27,910	7.66	74	10.97	68
Dumna	91,685	9.31	90	17.47	109
Kabirpanthi	37,623	16.99	167	29.63	186
Mazhabi	9,62,546	6.52	56	8.31	43
Megh	52,608	11.90	116	23.53	147
Sansi	39,084	8.20	79	11.01	68

Source: D'Souza, 1980.

ranging from 31 and 175 in 1961 and from 37 and 189 in 1971. Thus, whereas the educational inequalities between the Scheduled Castes and the rest of the population are narrowing down, even though very slowly, those among the Scheduled Castes *inter se* are widening.

I shall now illustrate how regional disparities and hierarchical inequalities are the major causes of the growing inequalities among the Scheduled Castes of Punjab. To take up regional disparities first, it may be pointed out that just as there is a high degree of variation in the educational level of the population of different states (as discussed above), there is also a higher degree of variation in the educational level of the population of the different districts of Punjab. For instance, in 1961, the percentage of literacy in Punjab varied from 18.7 in Sangrur district to 35.6 in Ludhiana district. There was also a similar variation in the percentage of literacy among the Scheduled Castes from 5.5 in Sangrur to 16.62 in Hoshiarpur. What is significant is that there is a high degree of correlation between the percentage of literacy in the total population and that in the Scheduled Caste population of a district, the coefficients of rank difference correlation in 1961, 1971 and 1981 being 0.845, 0.834 and 0.923 respectively. In other words, the chances of educational development of the Scheduled Castes of a district are very much bound up with the overall educational development of the district. They have better chances in districts which are, on the whole, better developed in education.

The districts may be compared (see Table 3.5) in terms of the educational attainments of their Scheduled Caste population in relation to the educational level of the Scheduled Caste population of the state. The relevant index of educational inequality is obtained as follows:

$$\text{IEE Scheduled Caste population of a district} = \frac{\text{\% of literate Scheduled Caste population of a district}}{\text{\% of literate Scheduled Caste population of the state}} \times 100$$

Table 3.5
Educational Inequalities among the Scheduled Castes of Different Districts
in Punjab, 1961, 1971 and 1981

District	IEE Scores		
	1961	1971	1981
Gurdaspur	97	118	124
Amritsar	86	75	73
Firozpur	65	52	51
Ludhiana	135	129	130
Jalandhar	147	152	150
Kapurthala	102	98	120
Hoshiarpur	157	181	174
Rupnagar	115	153	148
Patiala	78	79	85
Sangrur	54	56	57
Bhatinda	55	38	39
Faridkot*	—	—	52
Punjab	100	100	100

* Faridkot was included in Firozpur in 1961 and 1971.
Source: *Census of India*, Special Tables for Scheduled Castes, 1961 and 1971, and Primary Census Abstract, Scheduled Castes, 1981.

First, it can be seen that at every point of time there is a wide variation in the scores on the index of educational equality of the Scheduled Castes in the different districts, the range of variation being 103, 143 and 135 in 1961, 1971 and 1981 respectively. Even though there is a marginal decline in the range in 1981 as compared with 1971, the difference between the educationally least developed and the most developed districts is extremely large.

It is still more remarkable that the relative positions of the different districts with regard to the educational inequalities of the Scheduled Castes have remained almost the same over two decades. The coefficients of correlation of the IEE scores of the districts between 1961 and 1971, between 1971 and 1981 and between 1961 and 1981 were 0.989, 0.992 and 0.987 respectively. All these facts show how strongly the developmental chances of the Scheduled Castes are dependent upon the development of the region in which they are residing.

Another important aspect of the regional distribution is the fact that the different Scheduled Castes of a state are not uniformly distributed (relative to their proportion to the total) in every district, but are differentially distributed in the various districts. Among the eleven large and medium-sized Scheduled Castes, not more than five castes are concentrated in any single district (D'Souza, 1980; p. 35). Thus the districts of Gurdaspur and Firozpur have a concentration of five castes each; at the other extreme, Ludhiana has only one such caste while Hoshiarpur has two of them. Because of such an uneven distribution of the Scheduled Castes in different districts, it is obvious that the castes residing in districts with a higher level of educational development have a better chance of educational development as compared to those residing in districts which are less developed.

Having looked at the effect of regional disparities on educational inequalities among the Scheduled Castes, let us now examine the contribution of social hierarchies. Various studies of the social grading of castes discussed in Chapter 2 show that when two or more Scheduled Castes reside in a village or town, they are graded in a hierarchy of prestige and such a hierarchy is correlated to their economic hierarchy. Educational variation generally corresponds to the prestige hierarchy of castes.

In my 1980 study, when two or more castes are found concentrated in the same district, they also invariably form a social hierarchy which is related to their pronounced educational differences. The fact that educational differences are negatively correlated to the differences in the percentage of agricultural workers would indicate a correlation between education and the economic level of the Scheduled Castes residing in a district (D'Souza, 1980; pp. 41–42).

Since the Scheduled Castes residing in the same district occupy different positions in the social hierarchy, they have differential opportunities of educational development within the district. Thus the opportunities of a caste for educational development are not only governed by its residence in a district but also by its position in the social hierarchy of Scheduled Castes of the district. Because of this combined influence of regional disparities and social hierarchy, it can be deduced that the Scheduled Caste which resides in the district with the highest educational level of the Scheduled Castes and occupies the highest position in the social hierarchy of Scheduled Castes would have the best chances of educational advancement; conversely, the Scheduled Caste which resides in the district with the lowest educational level of the Scheduled Castes, and occupies the lowest position in the social hierarchy of the Scheduled Castes of that district would have the least chances of educational development. Since with educational development, in general, the regional disparities as well as hierarchical inequalities tend to increase, the educational inequalities between the most advanced and the least advanced Scheduled Castes of a state would keep on increasing.

The data presented in Table 3.6 show that the deductions following from our analysis are in fact true. The data are taken from the 1971 Census and, for the sake of homogeneity, are confined to the rural Scheduled Caste population.

In this table, the literacy percentages of each of the eleven large and medium-sized castes are shown under the districts in which they are concentrated, by arranging both the caste and the district in descending order of percentage of literacy among the Scheduled Castes. The underlying assumption in the presentation of data in this form is that the educational attainment of a given Scheduled Caste includes the structural effect of the region (district) as well as that of the caste hierarchy. That there is a combined effect of both the structural principles is revealed by the fact that the castes tend to be clustered along the diagonal cells in such a way that

Table 3.6

District-wise Percentages of Literacy among the Rural Population of Eleven Scheduled Castes in the Punjab

Caste	Hoshiarpur (28.99)	Ropar (23.99)	Jalandhar (23.34)	Ludhiana (20.35)	Gurdaspur (18.06)	Kapurthala (14.19)	Patiala (11.45)	Amritsar (10.30)	Sangrur (8.25)	Firozpur (7.04)	Bhatinda (4.81)
Kabirpanthi (28.95)	32.80	30.30	—	—	25.14	—	—	22.51	—	—	—
Ad-Dharmi (26.92)	30.28	—	24.98	—	—	21.47	—	—	—	—	—
Chamar (18.88)	—	26.64	—	22.75	—	—	13.56	—	9.70	—	—
Megh (17.03)	—	—	29.92	—	23.28	—	—	—	—	7.02	—
Dumna (16.56)	—	—	—	—	16.29	—	—	—	—	—	—
Balmiki (11.56)	—	17.24	15.06	—	12.15	8.41	8.82	—	—	4.32	—
Sansi (11.51)	—	—	—	—	13.86	—	—	9.20	4.34	—	—
Mazhabi (11.05)	—	—	—	—	—	—	—	9.81	—	6.03	4.07
Bazigar (7.34)	—	—	—	—	—	8.39	5.00	—	—	—	2.36
Bauria (6.42)	—	—	—	—	—	—	—	—	—	5.83	5.29
Dhanak (5.94)	—	—	—	—	—	—	—	—	2.75	7.54	4.95

Source: D'Souza, 1980.

Note: The castes as well as the districts are arranged in descending order of their percentages of literacy (shown in brackets).

those with a higher educational attainment are found located at the top left-hand corner and those with a lower educational attainment at the bottom right-hand corner; the former benefit doubly from their favourable location both in the regional context and the caste hierarchy, and the latter lose on both counts.

Except for the last two districts, in every district the Scheduled Castes form a hierarchy in their percentages of literacy. In the last two districts, however, where the hierarchy is disturbed, all the castes are of a smaller literacy level. Similarly, except for the caste at the bottom of the caste hierarchy, every caste has diminishing attainments as we move from districts with higher levels of literacy to districts with lower levels of literacy. Such a regular pattern (with minor discrepancies) would leave no one in doubt about the combined effect of regional disparities and hierarchical inequalities on the educational attainment of the Scheduled Castes in the Punjab. Since both kinds of inequalities are liable to increase with development, the educational inequalities among the Scheduled Castes *inter se* are also widening.

Attention has been focused in this chapter on the relative stability of two major types of structural inequalities—those related to spatial (territorial) structure and those related to social structure. When growth takes place, both these types of inequalities tend to become accentuated. Under certain conditions the two types of inequalities tend to reinforce each other.

4

Development and the Scheduled Castes: Inter-State Disparities

Socio-economic disparities affect most those people who are at the bottom of the scale—those who are below the poverty line. That poverty itself is largely a social-structural phenomenon is brought out by the fact that, in India, the overwhelming majority of the Scheduled Castes and Scheduled Tribes is poor. The Scheduled Castes, no matter where they are, are placed at the bottom of the caste hierarchy, and hence they enjoy very little prestige and economic security. Their low position in the social hierarchy is rendered all the more vulnerable because of the stigma of untouchability attached to them in the past and from which they are still not free in many places, especially in the rural areas.

Whereas the Scheduled Castes suffer due to their marginal position in the social hierarchy, the Scheduled Tribes are handicapped on account of their territorial marginality. The Scheduled Tribes are mostly people who are driven to the inaccessible hilly terrain to eke out a precarious economic existence. Because of their isolation from the social mainstream, they have been bypassed by the frontiers of modern civilization. With the new-found discovery of the resources of the hills and forests, the Scheduled Tribes inhabiting these areas have been brought increasingly into contact with people of the mainstream where they find themselves at the bottom of the socio-economic hierarchy of the larger society, sometimes occupying an economic position even lower than that of the Scheduled Castes.

Both the Scheduled Castes and Scheduled Tribes have been poor from time immemorial. If we disregard the effect of genetic factors which operate more or less in the same way in all population categories, it becomes abundantly clear that the perpetual back-wardness of these sections is due to the fact that they occupy marginal positions in the Indian social structure. In fact, the social-structural marginality of these people has been publicly recognized inasmuch as the Constitution of India has laid down directives to the governments for their uplift, and their present appellation of Scheduled Castes and Scheduled Tribes stems from this public concern.

A large number of state measures, popularly known as protective discrimination, have been introduced in order to give the Scheduled Castes and Scheduled Tribes a head-start so that they can make up for the oppression and neglect suffered by them in the past. In our global analysis it is not necessary to go into these details, especially when there are excellent accounts available on the subject (e.g., Galanter, 1984). Our main objective is to see the overall impact of these measures, as well as of development planning at large, on the development of these underprivileged sections.

It may be assumed that left to itself, without any interference of the developmental agencies, the society would change according to a pattern determined by the forces inherent in the social structure. Even when there is a general advancement, the relative positions of the different sections would remain more or less the same.

Development, on the other hand, would mean a structural transformation. Insofar as the Scheduled Castes and the Scheduled Tribes are concerned, development would mean their relative advancement. Instead of remaining always at the bottom, with development they would begin to climb the social ladder. Here it may be necessary to make a distinction between growth and development in the light of our discussion in Chapter 1. For example, the increase in education, urbanization and industriali-zation of the Scheduled Castes may contribute towards their growth in modernization; however, socio-structurally, they may still remain at the bottom if, in the meantime, the rest of the population also has grown equally fast or faster in the variables of modernization. In order that the growth of the Scheduled Castes be regarded as their development, in their growth they should have an edge over the rest of the population. Therefore, whereas mere growth of the Scheduled Castes may be denoted by the percentage increase in a given variable, their development may be gauged by their score on the index of equality in the given variable. As already mentioned in Chapter 3, the score of the Scheduled Castes on the index of equality in a variable (IEV) is obtained as follows:

$$IEV = \frac{\text{Percentage of Scheduled Castes in the variable}}{\text{Percentage of the rest of the population in the variable}} \times 100$$

The data for our analysis are taken from the 1961, 1971 and 1981 Census results. The year 1961 represents the initial phase of development planning in India, when its impact could have been barely visible; by 1981, the results of planning should be fully evident. The analysis consists of finding out the regional disparities of the Scheduled Castes or Scheduled Tribes in the crucial variables of modernization, and in relating these patterns to the variables of economic development and other relevant factors. The idea is to see, if economic development cannot fully account for the patterns of regional disparities, whether the structural dimensions would provide the answer. In this manner it is proposed to determine the relative importance of economic development and the structural factors in the development of the underprivileged sections of the Indian society.

For a regional analysis, only the larger states (i.e., states with not less than 1 per cent of the total population of the country) have been considered with a view to maintain relative uniformity among the units. Among the 15 such states, Assam—where census was not taken in 1981—has been omitted.

The variables of modernization which are considered are literacy, urbanization and the percentage of non-agricultural workers, which are the proxies for the typical variables of modernization (such as, education, urbanization and industrialization, respectively). Accordingly, the abbreviations IEE, IEU and IEI stand for the indexes of equality in education, urbanization and industrialization respectively, although IEE is worked out from the data on literacy and IEI from the information on non-agricultural workers.

In this chapter, we shall consider the growth and development of the Scheduled Castes in the 14 larger states (13 states in 1961) of the country. First, their growth and development in the variables of modernization will be related to the overall growth of the region, which will be indicated by two sets of variables, one set consisting of the per capita domestic product, and the other, the growth of the population other than the Scheduled Castes, in a given variable. Such an analysis would give an idea of the influence of development planning as a whole on the growth and development of the Scheduled Castes. Second, the growth and development of the Scheduled Castes will be related to some structural dimensions as represented by the percentages of the population of the Scheduled Castes and Scheduled Tribes. The structural implications of population sizes will be made clear in due course.

Pattern of Educational Growth and Development

Keeping the foregoing statements in mind, we shall now examine the relevant data drawn mainly from the 1961, 1971 and 1981 Census publications. First, the variable of education will be discussed in terms of literacy. Since the majority of the population in India is still illiterate, the literacy rate can be taken as an effective differentiating feature of the growth and development of the different population categories. The percentage of literate persons among the Scheduled Castes and the rest of the population (non-Scheduled Castes) and the scores on the index of educational equality (IEE) for the Scheduled Castes in the larger states of India are given in Tables 4.1, 4.2 and 4.3 for 1961, 1971 and 1981 respectively.

Educational Growth: The data presented in the tables reveal the wide difference in the literacy backgrounds of the Scheduled Caste and non-Scheduled Caste population over time. In 1961, whereas the percentage of literacy among the non-Scheduled Castes was 23.31, among the Scheduled Castes it was only 10.27; the corresponding percentages were 31.98 and 14.67 in 1971, and 39.01 and 21.38 in 1981. However, among both the sections there has been a steady growth of literacy over the decades, although the progress falls far short of the constitutional mandate to wipe out illiteracy within ten years of the adoption of the Constitution of free India.

An important aspect of the distribution of literacy rates is the wide variation in literacy percentages of the Scheduled Castes in the various states, decade after decade. This phenomenon is also shared by the non-Scheduled Castes. Kerala has consistently held the highest position in Scheduled Caste literacy at all the three

Table 4.1
Percentage of Literate Persons among the Scheduled Castes
and Non-Scheduled Castes and the Scores on the IEE for the Scheduled Castes
in the Larger States of India (1961)

State	% of Literate SCs		% of Literate Non-SCs		IEE Scores	
	% (1)	Rank (2)	% (3)	Rank (4)	Score (5)	Rank (6)
Andhra Pradesh	8.47	9	23.23	9	36	9
Bihar	5.96	13	20.36	11	29	13
Gujarat	22.46	2	31.02	4	72	1
Karnataka*	9.06	8	27.89	7	32	12
Kerala	24.44	1	48.97	1	50	3
Madhya Pradesh	7.89	10	18.53	12	43	5
Maharashtra	15.78	3	30.65	5	51	2
Orissa	11.57	6	23.55	8	49	4
Punjab†	9.64	7	27.95	6	34	11
Rajasthan	6.44	12	16.96	13	38	8
Tamil Nadu	14.66	4	35.07	2	42	6
Uttar Pradesh	7.14	11	20.39	10	35	10
West Bengal	13.58	5	32.99	3	41	7
India	10.27		23.31		39	

Source: *Census of India*, 1961, General Population Tables and Special Tables for Scheduled Castes.
* Known as Mysore in 1961.
† Includes the state of Haryana which was carved out in 1966.

points of time—1961, 1971 and 1981—while Bihar has held the lowest position all the while. It can also be seen that while the overall percentage of literacy has increased from 1961 to 1981, the range between the highest and the lowest percentages in states has widened; it has increased from 18 in 1961 to 34 in 1971 and 46 in 1981.

A similar pattern is also visible in the distribution of the literacy rates among the non-Scheduled Castes, but with varying details. For example, here the least literate state is Rajasthan and not Bihar as in the case of the Scheduled Castes.

In terms of these rough indices of inequality, it would appear that the inter-state educational inequalities have widened during the period of planned development, which have no doubt contributed to the overall growth of literacy or education. However,

Table 4.2

*Percentage of Literate Persons among the Scheduled Castes
and Non-Scheduled Castes and the Scores on the IEE for the Scheduled Castes
in the Larger States of India (1971)*

State	% of Literate SCs		% of Literate Non-SCs		IEE Scores	
	% (1)	Rank (2)	% (3)	Rank (4)	Score (5)	Rank (6)
Andhra Pradesh	10.66	11	26.70	10	40	13
Bihar	6.53	14	22.14	13	29	14
Gujarat	27.74	2	36.38	6	76	1
Haryana	12.60	9	30.22	8	42	9
Karnataka	13.89	8	34.19	7	41	12
Kerala	40.21	1	62.25	1	65	2
Madhya Pradesh	12.49	10	23.60	12	53	5
Maharashtra	25.27	3	40.70	3	63	3
Orissa	15.61	7	28.06	9	56	4
Punjab	16.12	6	39.42	4	41	11
Rajasthan	9.14	13	20.94	14	44	8
Tamil Nadu	21.82	4	43.27	2	50	6
Uttar Pradesh	10.20	12	24.76	11	41	10
West Bengal	17.80	5	37.03	5	48	7
India	14.67		31.98		46	

Source: *Census of India*, 1971, Union Primary Census Abstract and Special Tables
for Scheduled Castes.

when we consider inequality in the overall pattern of distribution, which can be obtained by the coefficient of relative variation (CRV)*, we find a less inegalitarian distribution emerging in 1981. The CRV figures for the Scheduled Castes during 1961, 1971 and 1981 are 47.2, 50.6 and 46.6 respectively, and for the non-Scheduled Castes are 28.6, 31.6 and 28.3 respectively. All the same, the inequalities are quite marked, and it is also obvious that the regional disparities in education are much sharper among the Scheduled Castes than among the non-Scheduled Castes.

The rigid character of the regional inequalities in the education of the Scheduled Castes is brought out by the fact that throughout the period considered, the ranks of the various states according to

$$* \quad \text{CRV} = \frac{\text{Standard deviation}}{\text{Mean}} \times 100$$

Table 4.3

Percentage of Literate Persons among the Scheduled Castes
and Non-Scheduled Castes and the Scores on the IEE for the Scheduled Castes
in the Larger States of India (1981)

State	% of Literate SCs		% of Literate Non-SCs		IEE Scores	
	% (1)	Rank (2)	% (3)	Rank (4)	Score (5)	Rank (6)
Andhra Pradesh	17.64	11	32.09	10	55	7
Bihar	10.40	14	28.89	13	36	14
Gujarat	39.79	2	44.00	6	90	1
Haryana	20.15	9	39.91	8	50	11
Karnataka	20.59	8	41.63	7	49	12
Kerala	55.96	1	72.03	1	78	2
Madhya Pradesh	18.97	10	29.34	12	65	4
Maharashtra	35.55	3	48.07	3	74	3
Orissa	22.41	7	36.26	9	62	5
Punjab	23.85	6	47.11	4	51	10
Rajasthan	14.05	13	26.51	14	53	8
Tamil Nadu	29.67	4	50.60	2	59	6
Uttar Pradesh	14.96	12	30.42	11	49	12
West Bengal	24.37	5	45.60	5	53	8
India	21.38		39.01		55	

Source: *Census of India*, 1981, Primary Census Abstract, General Population, and
Scheduled Castes.

the percentage of literacy among the Scheduled Castes have
remained almost the same; in fact, between 1971 and 1981 they
have maintained identical patterns. This observation holds good in
the case of the region-based educational inequalities among the
non-Scheduled Castes as well.

It is difficult to fathom the causes of these disparities, based as
they are on historical and other complex factors. But one can find
out some of their correlates and indicate whether development
planning, which has been in operation on several fronts, has affected
these educational disparities in any way. One of the variables
which is highly correlated with the regional variation in the literacy
rate of the Scheduled Castes is the literacy rate of the non-Scheduled
Castes (relationship between columns 2 and 4 in Tables 4.1, 4.2 and
4.3). The coefficients of correlation* between the regional variation

* These and most other coefficients of correlation subsequently used are
calculated according to the rank-difference correlation method.

in literacy among the Scheduled Castes and that among the non-Scheduled Castes are 0.902, 0.916 and 0.916 during 1961, 1971 and 1981 respectively, which are all very high. These relationships would suggest that the educational prospects of the Scheduled Castes in a region are inextricably linked with those of the rest of the population. Consequently, the educational inequalities of the Scheduled Castes in different regions are, to a large extent, based on the educational inequalities of the rest of the population.

The correlation between the educational levels of the Scheduled Castes and the non-Scheduled Castes is not a perfect one; there are a few notable discrepancies, which are especially observable in states such as Gujarat, Madhya Pradesh, Orissa, Punjab and Tamil Nadu, which have persisted over the decades. The reasons for these discrepancies will be made clear presently.

Insofar as development planning in India is primarily aimed at economic development, one would expect that the growth in literacy would also be correlated with the growth of the economy. One of the popularly used indices of the overall economic development of a state is its per capita domestic product (PCDP). The ranks of the various states based on their literacy rates and PCDP, both for the Scheduled Castes and the non-Scheduled Castes, are shown in Table 4.4 for 1961 and Table 4.5 for 1971 and 1981. The correlation between the literacy rate and PCDP for Scheduled Castes and non-Scheduled Castes over different points of time is summarized as follows:

Variables Correlated with PCDP	Coefficients of Correlation		
	1961	*1971*	*1981*
Literacy rates of Scheduled Castes in states	0.559	0.578	0.670
Literacy rates of non-Scheduled Castes in states	0.610	0.649	0.705

The results show that educational growth is positively affected by economic growth, although the relevant coefficients of correlation are of a moderately high degree. There is, however, a consistent pattern in the correlations between the Scheduled Castes and non-Scheduled Castes over the decades. At every decadal point of time, the coefficient is relatively stronger among the

Table 4.4

States Ranked according to the Per Capita Domestic Product and Literacy Rate of the Scheduled Castes and of the Rest of the Population (1961)

State	Rank on Literacy Rate		Rank on Per Capita
	SCs	Non-SCs	Domestic Product
Andhra Pradesh	9	9	6
Bihar	10	11	12
Gujarat	3	4	4
Karnataka	6	7	6
Kerala	1	1	8
Madhya Pradesh	12	12	10
Maharashtra	4	5	2
Orissa	8	8	13
Punjab	7	6	1
Rajasthan	13	13	9
Tamil Nadu	2	2	5
Uttar Pradesh	11	10	11
West Bengal	5	3	3

Source: *Census of India*, 1961, General Population Tables, and Special Tables for Scheduled Castes; and Dandekar, 1988.

non-Scheduled Castes as compared with the Scheduled Castes. Further, both among the Scheduled Castes and non-Scheduled Castes, the coefficients have increased in strength over the years. Therefore, there can be no doubt that the educational growth of both the Scheduled Castes and non-Scheduled Castes of a region is to some extent related to the economic growth of that region. The coefficients of correlation in this case would have been much higher but for some pronounced discrepancies found in some states. In 1961, the educational levels of both the Scheduled Castes and non-Scheduled Castes in Kerala were far ahead of the economic level of the state; the reverse was the case in Punjab (Table 4.4). Similarly, both in 1971 and 1981 Haryana and Punjab had far lower educational levels and Kerala far higher educational levels both among the Scheduled Castes and non-Scheduled Castes compared with the economic growth of the states (Table 4.5).

These major discrepancies between economic growth and educational levels show that mere economic development, as measured by the growth of the domestic product, does not automatically lead to educational progress and much less to the educational growth of the Scheduled Castes.

Table 4.5

States Ranked according to the Per Capita Domestic Product and Literacy Rate
of the Scheduled Castes and of the Rest of the Population (1971–81)

State	Rank on Literacy Rates in 1971 and 1981*		Ranks on Per Capita Domestic Product	
	Scheduled Castes	Other Population	1971	1981
Andhra Pradesh	11	10	10	9
Bihar	14	13	14	14
Gujarat	2	6	3	4
Haryana	9	8	2	2
Karnataka	8	7	6	6
Kerala	1	1	7	7
Madhya Pradesh	10	12	13	11
Maharashtra	3	3	4	3
Orissa	7	9	11	10
Punjab	6	4	1	1
Rajasthan	13	14	8	12
Tamil Nadu	4	2	9	8
Uttar Pradesh	12	11	12	13
West Bengal	5	5	5	5

Source: *Census of India*, Union Primary Census Abstract and Special Tables for
Scheduled Castes, 1971, and Primary Census Abstract, General Popu-
lation, and Scheduled Castes, 1981.
* These ranks were the same in 1971 and 1981.

However, one of the major findings which emerges from the
data presented so far is that although development planning has
contributed to the growth of education among both the Scheduled
Castes and non-Scheduled Castes, it has not been able to bring
about any perceptible transformation in the inequalitarian distribution of educational levels in the various states both among the
Scheduled Castes and non-Scheduled Castes; the same pattern of
distribution which was prevalent at the initial phase of planning in
1961 has, by and large, persisted in 1971 and 1981 as well. The
reasons for this will be considered later.

Educational Development: Absolute growth in literacy or education
does not provide us with a satisfactory index of true development.
True development for the Scheduled Castes would mean liberation
from their position at the bottom of society. A rise in their literacy
rates does not give an indication of this kind of development,
which is better reflected in the index of educational equality (IEE).

The scores on the IEE for the Scheduled Castes (Tables 4.1, 4.2 and 4.3, column 5) provide a comparative picture of the relative educational deprivation of the Scheduled Castes in the different states in 1961, 1971 and 1981. The scores have increased from 39 in 1961, to 46 in 1971 and 55 in 1981. At the aggregative level, even in 1981 the Scheduled Castes have advanced in literacy only to the extent of about 55 per cent of the advancement of the non-Scheduled Castes; they still have to go a long way to attain parity in literacy with the non-Scheduled Castes. Nevertheless, they have made steady progress in this respect from 1961.

On the whole, therefore, the Scheduled Castes have been able to reduce the gap existing between their own educational level and that of the non-Scheduled Castes, to some extent. But the relative deprivation of the Scheduled Castes in the different states is not of the same order and it is with this aspect that we are more concerned. Indeed, at every point of time, there is a wide variation in the scores on the index of educational equality. In 1961 (Table 4.1, column 5), the IEE scores ranged from 29 in Bihar to 72 in Gujarat, with a range of 43. In 1971 (Table 4.2) and 1981 (Table 4.3) also, the same states—Bihar and Gujarat—were at the bottom and the top of the range respectively; the range had even widened from 43 in 1981 to 47 in 1971 and 54 in 1981. Whereas the distance between the states with the highest and the lowest IEE scores has increased, the coefficient of relative variation (CRV) has declined somewhat; from 24.83 in 1961, the coefficient has come down to 24.24 in 1971 and 22.94 in 1981.

Apart from the fact that the differences between the IEE scores among the states (at any rate, between the states with the highest and the lowest IEE scores) have increased, the relative ranks of the states in terms of these states have also remained largely the same from 1961 to 1981, the relevant coefficients of correlation being as follows:

Years for which Ranks are Correlated	Coefficients of Correlation
1961 and 1971	0.967
1971 and 1981	0.892
1961 and 1981	0.962

It would, therefore, appear that whereas development planning has been able to reduce somewhat the relative deprivation of the

Scheduled Castes in literacy in overall terms, it has not been able to do away with the regional inequalities in this respect.

As one might expect there is a high degree of correlation between the IEE scores of the Scheduled Castes in a state and their percentage of literacy. These correlations for 1961, 1971 and 1981 are 0.604, 0.850 and 0.729. In other words, states in which the Scheduled Castes have shown higher growth in education have progressed better in achieving a higher degree of parity of education for the Scheduled Castes as compared with the non-Scheduled Castes.

On the other hand, the relationship between the IEE scores of the Scheduled Castes and the rate of literacy of the non-Scheduled Castes is rather low, the relevant coefficients of correlation for the years 1961, 1971 and 1981 being 0.456, 0.475 and 0.455 respectively. As a matter of fact, the coefficients in this case should have been even lower inasmuch as the parity in education for Scheduled Castes would depend upon their educational growth surpassing that of the non-Scheduled Castes. But interestingly, as we have already seen, the educational progress of the Scheduled Castes also depends upon the educational progress of their non-Scheduled Caste compatriots, which may be broadly equated with the educational development of the region.

With a view to ascertain the influence of economic development upon the educational equality of the Scheduled Castes, the ranks of the states on the IEE scores of the Scheduled Castes are correlated with their ranks on the PCDP (per capita domestic product) as an index of economic development. The coefficients of correlation in this case turn out to be negligible, being 0.176, 0.222 and 0.233 for the years 1961, 1971 and 1981 respectively. This piece of evidence would come as a great disappointment to those who maintain that economic development is the solution to many of our social ills.

Thus, whereas the general educational growth of a region as well as its economic growth greatly influence the educational growth of the Scheduled Castes, their influence upon the educational development (equality) of the Scheduled Castes is much less (in fact, negligible on the part of economic development). There appear to be other important variables whose effects seem to countervail the effect of regional growth upon the educational equality or educational development of the Scheduled Castes. We shall return to this issue after examining the patterns of their urban and industrial development.

Pattern of Urban Growth and Development

It is generally assumed that education, urbanization and indus-trialization in a developing society are interrelated and, in Chapter 3, we have shown that this is true of India as well. Consequently, one would expect that the patterns of urban growth and develop-ment of the Scheduled Castes would be similar to those of their educational growth and development, which we have just examined. We may, therefore, analyse the urban pattern in the same way we have analysed the educational pattern, and wherever appropriate we may call attention to the similarities and dissimilarities between the urban and educational patterns of growth and development.

As in literacy rate, so also in urbanization the Scheduled Castes lag far behind the rest of the population, as shown below:

Population Category	Urban %		
	1961	*1971*	*1981*
Scheduled Castes	10.70	11.94	16.00
Non-Scheduled Castes	19.20	21.27	25.14

At every point of time, the percentage of the urban population among the Scheduled Castes is far less than that among the non-Scheduled Castes. But the growth rates which are shown below provide some evidence of these gaps narrowing down:

Population Category	Growth in the percentage of urban population %	
	1961–71	*1971–81*
Scheduled Castes	11.59	34.10
Non-Scheduled Castes	10.78	18.19

The rate of urbanization (which was relatively low and almost even between the two categories) became much faster during 1971–81 and was particularly high among the Scheduled Castes.

A detailed analysis of the regional inequalities in the growth and development of urbanization among the Scheduled Castes and non-Scheduled Castes follows.

Urban Growth: The percentage distribution of the urban population among the Scheduled Castes and non-Scheduled Castes and the index scores on urban equality (IEU)* of the Scheduled Castes, according to the larger states in the country, is shown in Tables 4.6, 4.7 and 4.8 for the census years 1961, 1971 and 1981 respectively. We have already seen in the foregoing the aggregative trends in urbanization showing a much lower level of representation of the Scheduled Castes in the urban areas. When expressed in IEU scores, the aggregate urban representation of Scheduled Castes in 1961, 1971 and 1981 (shown in Tables 4.6, 4.7 and 4.8) turns out to be 56, 56 and 64. Their urban representation in the country (which was just 56 and was constant both in 1961 and 1971) suddenly showed a spurt in 1981, which is consistent with the relatively much higher rate of urban growth of Scheduled Castes from 1971–81. The Scheduled Castes are still represented only to the tune of about two-thirds of the level attained by the non-Scheduled Castes. Still the question remains, whether their much faster urban growth during 1971–81 is an index of their better developmental opportunity or the lack of it? We shall throw some light on this issue as we proceed.

In urbanization too, as in literacy rate, there is a high degree of variation both among the Scheduled Castes and non-Scheduled Castes at the three points of time—1961, 1971 and 1981 (Tables 4.6, 4.7 and 4.8, columns 1 and 3). Gujarat has always had the highest percentage of urban Scheduled Castes. The lowest rank in this respect was occupied by Orissa in 1961 and 1971 and by Bihar in 1981; Orissa held the last but one rank in 1981 just as Bihar filled this rank in the previous two decades.

The range of variation in the percentage of the Scheduled Caste population in the various states was 19.8, 20.96 and 24.21 in 1961, 1971 and 1981 respectively. In other words, in the increase in the overall rate of urbanization, the distribution of the percentage of urban people among the Scheduled Castes has become more

$$IEU = \frac{\text{Urban percentage among the SCs}}{\text{Urban percentage among the Non-SCs}} \times 100$$

Table 4.6

Percentage of the Urban Population among the Scheduled Castes and Non-Scheduled Castes and the Scores on the IEU for the Scheduled Castes in the Larger States of India (1961)

State	% of Urban SCs		% of Urban Non-SCs		IEU Scores	
	% (1)	Rank (2)	% (3)	Rank (4)	Score (5)	Rank (6)
Andhra Pradesh	11.1	7	18.4	7	60	8
Bihar	5.4	12	8.9	12	61	7
Gujarat	24.4	1	25.9	4	94	1
Karnataka	16.3	3	23.2	6	70	5
Kerala	8.5	10	15.7	9	56	9
Madhya Pradesh	10.7	8	14.8	10	72	4
Maharashtra	21.8	2	28.6	2	76	2
Orissa	4.6	13	6.6	13	69	6
Punjab	11.6	6	24.5	5	47	12
Rajasthan	12.3	5	16.7	8	73	3
Tamil Nadu	15.3	4	29.2	1	52	10
Uttar Pradesh	6.9	11	14.4	11	48	11
West Bengal	9.8	9	28.1	3	35	13
India	10.7		19.2		56	

Source: *Census of India*, 1961, General Population Tables, and Special Tables for Scheduled Castes.

unequal. However, the general pattern of inequalities as given by the CRV coefficients has become slightly less inegalitarian, the CRV coefficients for 1961, 1971 and 1981 being 48.2, 46.05 and 41.08 respectively.

The regional variation in urbanization is acute even in the case of the non-Scheduled Castes. In their case it is always Tamil Nadu which has held the first rank and Orissa the last. The range had varied from 22.6 in 1961 to 24.54 in 1971 and 23.61 in 1981. The coefficients of relative variation were 36.89, 34.28 and 29.20 in 1961, 1971 and 1981 respectively. An overall comparison of the Scheduled Castes and non-Scheduled Castes with regard to their pattern of urban population distribution would indicate that regional inequalities of urbanization are sharper among the Scheduled Castes than among the non-Scheduled Castes.

It would, therefore, appear that the inter-state inequalities in urbanization among the Scheduled Castes have widened during

Table 4.7

*Percentage of the Urban Population among the Scheduled Castes and
Non-Scheduled Castes and the Scores on the IEU for the Scheduled Castes
in the Larger States of India (1971)*

State	% of Urban SCs		% of Urban Non-SCs		IEU Scores	
	% (1)	Rank (2)	% (3)	Rank (4)	Score (5)	Rank (6)
Andhra Pradesh	11.81	8	20.36	7	58	8
Bihar	6.46	13	10.59	13	61	7
Gujarat	27.23	1	28.07	4	97	1
Haryana	10.39	9	19.24	8	54	11
Karnataka	16.80	4	25.27	6	66	6
Kerala	9.71	10	16.74	11	58	9
Madhya Pradesh	12.56	7	16.75	10	75	4
Maharashtra	24.69	2	31.65	2	78	2
Orissa	6.27	14	8.71	14	72	5
Punjab	14.70	5	25.79	5	57	10
Rajasthan	14.28	6	18.31	9	78	2
Tamil Nadu	17.29	3	33.25	1	52	12
Uttar Pradesh	7.56	12	15.75	12	48	13
West Bengal	8.20	11	29.28	3	28	14
India	11.94		21.27		56	

Source: *Census of India*, 1971, Union Primary Census Abstract, and Special Tables
for Scheduled Castes.

the period of planned development although the Scheduled Castes
have experienced appreciable urban growth during this period.
This trend, undoubtedly, counters the notion of justice implicit in
the concept of development.

Again, despite urban growth which was considerable (especially
during 1971–81), there has not been much change in the relative
ranks of the states on their percentages of urban Scheduled Caste
population. The correlation coefficients between the ranks in 1961
and 1971, and in 1971 and 1981 are 0.976 and 0.987, which stresses
the relative stability of the pattern of the percentages of urban
Scheduled Castes in the various states. Here, too, development
planning has not been able to bring about a desired mode of
transformation into the inegalitarian situation.

The inegalitarian pattern of distribution of the urban population
in the various states is also found among the non-Scheduled Castes

Table 4.8

Percentage of the Urban Population among the Scheduled Castes and
Non-Scheduled Castes and the Scores on the IEU for the Scheduled Castes
in the Larger States of India (1981)

State	% of Urban SCs		% of Urban Non-SCs		IEU Scores	
	% (1)	Rank (2)	% (3)	Rank (4)	Score (5)	Rank (6)
Andhra Pradesh	15.18	8	24.73	7	61	10
Bihar	8.48	14	13.15	13	64	7
Gujarat	32.69	1	30.98	3	106	1
Haryana	15.06	9	23.49	8	64	7
Karnataka	21.93	3	30.13	6	73	6
Kerala	12.14	11	19.51	12	62	9
Madhya Pradesh	17.92	7	20.69	10	87	3
Maharashtra	31.56	2	35.29	2	89	2
Orissa	9.40	13	12.22	14	77	5
Punjab	18.73	5	30.97	4	60	11
Rajasthan	17.95	6	21.63	9	83	4
Tamil Nadu	20.17	4	35.83	1	56	12
Uttar Pradesh	10.46	12	19.96	11	52	13
West Bengal	12.41	10	30.44	5	41	14
India	16.00		25.14		64	

Source: *Census of India*, 1981, Primary Census Abstract, General Population, and
Scheduled Castes.

and, to a large extent, it is correlated with the variation in the percentage of urban population among the Scheduled Castes, the coefficients of correlation for the years 1961, 1971 and 1981 being 0.786, 0.776 and 0.842 respectively. All the coefficients are high and the relationship has become stronger in 1981 when urban growth also showed a spurt. These relationships would imply that the opportunities of urbanization for the Scheduled Castes are governed, to some extent, by the opportunities of urbanization for the non-Scheduled Castes. However, the correlation between the opportunities of urbanization for the Scheduled Castes and the non-Scheduled Castes is not as high as the correlation between the educational opportunities for the Scheduled Castes and non-Scheduled Castes.

Urbanization is usually a consequence of economic development. When the ranks of the states on urbanization are correlated with those on the per capita domestic product (PCDP), the relevant coefficients of correlation for the years 1961, 1971 and 1981 turn out to be 0.714, 0.534 and 0.584 respectively. The corresponding correlations in the case of the non-Scheduled Castes are 0.906, 0.624 and 0.642. All the coefficients are of a moderate to high degree. It is interesting to note that both among the Scheduled Castes and non-Scheduled Castes the strengths of the correlations were far higher in 1961 than subsequently. Is one to conclude from these results that the growing urbanization since 1961 is not founded on the lines of sound economic development?

To sum up the findings regarding the pattern of urban growth of the Scheduled Castes, one may say that in their urbanization, the Scheduled Castes lag very much behind the rest of the population in every state. Their urban growth in the different states is extremely uneven but their regional disparities in urbanization are highly correlated with the regional disparities in the urbanization of the rest of the population. They are also correlated with the regional variations in the PCDP to a moderate to high degree. In other words, the urbanization of the Scheduled Castes in a state is promoted both by the overall urbanization and by the economic development of the state.

Urban Development: The pattern of urban development (IEE scores) of the Scheduled Castes, as we shall see, resembles the pattern of their urban growth (urban percentages) in certain respects and differs from it totally in certain other respects. As already pointed out, the Scheduled Castes have still to cover much ground before they can attain parity in urbanization with the non-Scheduled Castes (IEU score = 100), since their overall IEU score (which was only 56 both in 1961 and 1971) rose to 65 in 1981 (Tables 4.6, 4.7 and 4.8, column 5).

The IEU scores of the Scheduled Castes are highly uneven in the different states at all the three points of time—1961, 1971 and 1981. States such as Gujarat and Maharashtra depict an urban representation of the Scheduled Castes which is closer to that of the non-Scheduled Castes. However, in states such as West Bengal, Punjab and Uttar Pradesh, the Scheduled Castes are woefully under-represented in the urban areas. The ranges in the regional variation in the scores on IEU are as high as 59, 69, and 65 in 1961, 1971 and 1981 respectively. Although compared with 1971 the range has slightly decreased in 1981, it is still very high. The coefficients of relative variations for the years 1961, 1971 and 1981 are 23.64, 25.39 and 23.81 respectively.

Thus, even though the IEE score has increased, especially from 1971 to 1981 (which represents a situation favourable to the Scheduled Castes as compared with the non-Scheduled Castes), the regional inequalities have remained more or less the same. Still worse, the relative positions of the states in terms of their unequal ranks on the IEE scores have remained almost the same, the coefficients of correlation between the ranks in 1961 and 1971 and between 1971 and 1981 being 0.976 and 0.944 respectively. All this evidence calls attention to the rigidity of the inequalities which have proved to be beyond the ability of development planning as it is practised in India to break down.

However, when we come to the correlation between urban development (IEU) and urban growth (per cent urban) of the Scheduled Castes, we find that this relationship is rather weak, unlike the correlation between educational development and the educational growth of the Scheduled Castes which is very high. Whereas the coefficients of correlation between urban development (column 6 in Tables 4.6, 4.7 and 4.8) and urban growth (column 2 in these tables) are as low as 0.484, 0.413 and 0.409 in 1961, 1971 and 1981 respectively, those between educational development (column 6 in Tables 4.1, 4.2 and 4.3) and urban growth (column 2 in these tables) are 0.604, 0.850 and 0.729 in 1961, 1971 and 1981 respectively, which are consistently higher than those in the former series. This is rather unexpected. But what is still more unexpected is the fact that there is almost a total lack of relationship between urban development (IEU scores) of the Scheduled Castes and the overall urbanization of the state as represented by the level of urbanization of the non-Scheduled Castes (column 4 in Tables 4.6, 4.7 and 4.8). The coefficients of correlation between the IEU scores of the Scheduled Castes (column 6 in the tables) and the urban percentage of non-Scheduled Castes (column 4 in the tables) are 0.478, −0.084 and −0.031 in 1961, 1971 and 1981 respectively. Only in 1961, at the beginning of development planning, was there a moderate degree of relationship between the two variables. Therefore, development planning as such has played no significant role in contributing towards an equitable urban representation for the Scheduled Castes. This is further confirmed by the fact that the coefficients of correlation between the IEU scores and the PCDP (representing economic development) are negligible, being −0.110, −0.013 and 0.035 for the years 1961, 1971 and 1981 respectively.

This evidence shows that the Scheduled Castes on the whole are very much under-represented in the urban areas although over the years, especially from 1971 to 1981, there has been some improvement in this regard. But their urban representation is very uneven in the different states. This uenven representation, however, is influenced neither by the overall urbanization of the state nor by its economic development. There is hardly any modification of the pattern of uneven urban representation of the Scheduled Castes in the states brought about by economic development. Even the relationship between urban growth (per cent urban) and urban development (IEU scores) of the Scheduled Castes is rather low, the coefficients of correlation being 0.484, 0.413 and 0.419 in 1961, 1971 and 1981 respectively.

Pattern of Industrial Growth and Development

As already mentioned, industrialization has been operationally defined as the percentage of non-agricultural workers. This is a very coarse index of the growth of industry in a region. This index, in the initial stages of industrialization, can be very misleading since, during this period, the proportion of workers in the manufacturing industries, which is a more precise index of industrialization, may be relatively small among the non-agricultural workers.

Another aspect showing the coarseness of this index is the fact that whereas manufacturing industries may be broadly divided into household industries and other than household industries, economic development refers mainly to the growth of industries other than household ones. To make this distinction clear let us consider the following classification of industries for the census years 1961, 1971 and 1981:

Percentage of Workers in Broad Types of Manufacturing Industries

Year	Household Industries	Other than Household Industries	Total Manufacturing Industries
1961	6.38	4.22	10.60
1971	3.52	5.94	9.46
1981	3.46	7.83	11.29

It can be seen that, over the years, the percentage of household industries has been declining and that of industries other than household ones has been steadily increasing. But the aggregate picture is rather confusing. Such a distinction may be useful for interpreting some of the confusing trends which we might encounter in our analysis. It may be mentioned that, for practical considerations, we have not taken note of the definitional changes of workforce participation introduced by the census enumerators in 1971 and 1981, which may also vitiate our analysis to some extent.

Disregarding the coarseness of the index, we may denote the industrial growth of the Scheduled Castes by their percentage of non-agricultural workers, and their industrial development by the index of equality of industrialization (IEI) which is derived as follows:

$$\text{IEI} = \frac{\text{Percentage of non-agricultural workers among the SC workers}}{\text{Percentage of non-agricultural workers among the non-SC workers}} \times 100$$

In considering the industrial growth and development of the Scheduled Castes, one should bear in mind some of the basic differences in the occupational distribution of the Scheduled Castes and non-Scheduled Castes. If the occupations are divided into the three broad categories of cultivators, agricultural labourers and non-agricultural workers, as in Table 4.9, the Scheduled Castes (as compared with the non-Scheduled Castes) are grossly over-represented in the category of agricultural labourers which is at the bottom of the occupational-prestige ladder. They are under-represented in the categories of cultivators and non-agricultural workers. Both the categories of cultivators and non-agricultural workers are heterogeneous ones with regard to the prestige of workers. The Scheduled Castes, when they are included in these categories, are mostly found in occupations of lower prestige.

A decade-wise comparison of occupational distribution shown in Table 4.9 reveals that there has been a general deterioration in the occupational background of the people from 1961 to 1971 inasmuch as the category of cultivators has greatly shrunk and that of agricultural labourers has greatly expanded. This deterioration has affected the Scheduled Castes the most. The Scheduled Castes

Table 4.9
Percentage Distribution of Workers in the Total, Non-Scheduled Caste and
Scheduled Caste Populations according to Broad Occupational Categories
(1961, 1971 and 1981)

Population Category	Occupational Category		
	Cultivators	Agricultural Labourers	Non-Agricultural Workers
1961			
Total	52.81	16.71	30.48
Non-Scheduled Castes	54.88	13.24	31.88
Scheduled Castes	40.79	36.82	22.39
1971			
Total	43.34	26.33	30.33
Non-Scheduled Castes	46.31	21.44	32.25
Scheduled Castes	27.87	51.75	20.38
1981			
Total	41.58	24.94	33.48
Non-Scheduled Castes	44.33	20.17	35.50
Scheduled Castes	28.17	48.22	23.61

Source: *Census of India*, 1961, 1971, 1981, Tables for General Population and for
Scheduled Castes.

have also undergone a reduction in the category of non-agricultural
workers due mainly to an erosion in the occupational category of
household industry (not shown in the Table). From 1971 to 1981
the Scheduled Castes have shown some improvement in their
occupational background inasmuch as their percentage in the
agricultural labourer category has somewhat shrunk with a corresponding increase in the category of non-agricultural workers.

However, how far is this change a real improvement in their
economic situation cannot be inferred from these figures alone. It
is just possible that the combined effect of a growing population
and inelastic opportunities in agriculture has resulted in the purging
of an unusually large segment of the Scheduled Caste workers
from their employment as agricultural labourers. On the other
hand, there is ample evidence to show that the Scheduled Caste
workers are heavily concentrated in the low-paid jobs in the
informal part of the non-agricultural sector. Therefore, the
relatively better urban growth rate of the Scheduled Castes (to
which attention has already been drawn in the last section) cannot be
interpreted as a developmental gain accrued to the Scheduled Castes.

Industrial Growth: As in the case of education and urbanization, for the proxy variable of industrialization also there is a wide variation in the percentage of the Scheduled Castes in the various states which has persisted from 1961 to 1981 (Tables 4.10, 4.11 and 4.12). In 1961, Kerala stood first according to the percentage of non-agricultural workers among the Scheduled Castes, and Andhra Pradesh the last; in 1971 and 1981, Gujarat had overtaken Kerala to occupy the first position and Bihar had slid into the last position. The difference in the percentage between the least and the most industrially developed states had changed from 33.57 in 1961 to 23.7 in 1971 and to 29.26 in 1981. In the case of education and urbanization, the corresponding ranges had all increased over the years. The exception in this case between 1961 and 1971 may be attributed to the erosion of the household industries which was particularly heavy during this decade. Nevertheless, the percentages of non-agricultural workers in the different states are highly uneven.

Table 4.10

Percentage of Non-Agricultural Workers among the Scheduled Castes and Non-Scheduled Castes and the Scores on the IEI for the Scheduled Castes in the Larger States of India (1961)

State	Non-Agricultural Workers among SCs		Non-Agricultural Workers among Non-SCs		IEI Scores	
	% (1)	Rank (2)	% (3)	Rank (4)	Score (5)	Rank (6)
Andhra Pradesh	15.15	13	34.15	5	44	13
Bihar	17.88	12	22.91	10	78	7
Gujarat	33.31	4	31.81	6	105	3
Karnataka	19.42	9	18.91	13	103	4
Kerala	48.72	1	63.35	1	77	8
Madhya Pradesh	18.24	11	21.05	12	87	6
Maharashtra	22.93	7	30.47	7	75	9
Orissa	35.22	3	24.44	9	144	1
Punjab	42.61	2	34.60	4	135	2
Rajasthan	20.92	8	22.65	11	92	5
Tamil Nadu	23.48	6	43.16	3	54	11
Uttar Pradesh	18.53	10	26.63	8	70	10
West Bengal	24.68	5	50.90	2	48	12
India	22.39		31.87		70	

Source: *Census of India*, 1961, General Population Tables, and Special Tables for Scheduled Castes.

Table 4.11

Percentage of Non-Agricultural Workers among the Scheduled Castes and
Non-Scheduled Castes and the Scores on the IEI for the Scheduled Castes
in the Larger States of India (1971)

State	Non-Agricultural Workers among SCs		Non-Agricultural Workers among Non-SCs		IEI Scores	
	% (1)	Rank (2)	% (3)	Rank (4)	Score (5)	Rank (6)
Andhra Pradesh	14.2	13	33.0	9	43	13
Bihar	11.4	14	19.1	14	60	9
Gujarat	35.1	1	34.3	8	102	2
Haryana	33.5	2	35.0	6	96	4
Karnataka	25.0	7	34.8	7	72	8
Kerala	32.1	4	54.2	1	59	10
Madhya Pradesh	18.8	10	20.9	13	90	6
Maharashtra	32.3	3	35.3	5	92	5
Orissa	23.3	9	22.4	12	104	1
Punjab	31.3	5	39.3	4	80	7
Rajasthan	25.5	6	25.9	10	98	3
Tamil Nadu	17.8	11	43.6	3	41	14
Uttar Pradesh	14.4	12	25.1	11	57	11
West Bengal	24.0	8	46.1	2	52	12
India	20.4		32.2		63	

Source: *Census of India*, 1971, Union Primary Census Abstract, and Special Tables
for Scheduled Castes.

It may also be pointed out that the ranks of states according to
the percentages of non-agricultural workers among the Scheduled
Castes (column 2 in Tables 4.10, 4.11 and 4.12) remained relatively
stable over the decades. But here, again, the ranks were relatively
less stable between 1961 and 1971 ($r = 0.692$) as compared with
the ranks between 1971 and 1981 ($r = 0.973$). In the case of the
non-Scheduled Castes also, although the figures are different, the
same trends in the pattern of industrial growth are noticeable as
the ones described in the case of the Scheduled Castes. The
coefficients of relative variation for the distributions among the
Scheduled Castes for the years 1961, 1971 and 1981 are 38.34,
38.18 and 33.34 respectively and among the non-Scheduled Castes
are 35.80, 29.08 and 27.58 respectively. These values indicate that
the regional inequalities are sharper among the Scheduled Castes
than among the non-Scheduled Castes.

Table 4.12

Percentage of Non-Agricultural Workers among the Scheduled Castes and
Non-Scheduled Castes and the Scores on the IEI for the Scheduled Castes
in the Larger States of India (1981)

State	Non-Agricultural Workers among SCs		Non-Agricultural Workers among Non-SCs		IEI Scores	
	% (1)	Rank (2)	% (3)	Rank (4)	Score (5)	Rank (6)
Andhra Pradesh	14.35	13	33.94	9	42	13
Bihar	13.54	14	22.53	14	60	10
Gujarat	42.80	1	39.65	6	108	1
Haryana	36.86	4	39.77	5	93	5
Karnataka	26.44	8	36.69	8	72	8
Kerala	39.63	2	61.71	1	64	9
Madhya Pradesh	24.34	9	23.70	13	102	2
Maharashtra	37.53	3	38.43	7	98	3
Orissa	23.67	10	25.62	12	92	6
Punjab	33.31	5	45.09	3	74	7
Rajasthan	30.08	6	31.15	10	97	4
Tamil Nadu	18.84	11	44.55	4	42	13
Uttar Pradesh	17.32	12	29.93	11	58	11
West Bengal	27.16	7	50.33	2	54	12
India	23.16		35.50		66	

Source: *Census of India*, 1981, Primary Census Abstract, General Population, and
Scheduled Castes.

It has been broadly shown in Chapter 3 that modernization goes
with correlated changes in the growth of education, urbanization
and industrialization. How far is this true in the case of the
Scheduled Castes and the non-Scheduled Castes can be seen from
the following patterns of coefficients of correlation over the years:

Pairs of Variables Concerning Scheduled Castes	Coefficients of Correlation		
	1961	1971	1981
Per cent literate & per cent urban*	0.545	0.615	0.632
Per cent literate & per cent non-agricultural workers	0.741	0.731	0.683
Per cent urban and per cent non-agricultural workers*	0.201	0.574	0.637

Pairs of Variables Concerning Non-Scheduled Castes	Coefficients of Correlation		
	1961	1971	1981
Per cent literate & per cent urban*	0.811	0.841	0.852
Per cent literate & per cent non-agricultural workers	0.791	0.888	0.850
Per cent urban and per cent non-agricultural workers*	0.622	0.884	0.802

* Excludes Kerala.

It is obvious from these patterns of coefficients of correlation between the pairs of variables of modernization that the relationships between the variables have become stronger in 1971 and 1981 as compared with 1961, implying thereby that the correlations have become stronger with the advancement of development planning. Secondly, it can be seen that in every case the corresponding coefficient of correlation is stronger among the non-Scheduled Castes than among the Scheduled Castes. This implies that modernization has been more effective among the non-Scheduled Castes than among the Scheduled Castes.

The industrial growth of the Scheduled Castes is correlated to a moderate to high degree with the regional industrial growth (percentage of non-agricultural workers among the non-Scheduled Caste workers) as well as with the per capita domestic product of the state in 1961, 1971 and 1981. The relevant coefficients of correlation are as follows:

Pairs of Variables Correlated	Coefficients of Correlation		
	1961	1971	1981
Per cent non-agricultural workers among the Scheduled Castes and non-Scheduled Castes	0.560	0.494	0.617
Per cent non-agricultural workers among the Scheduled Castes and the PCDP of the state	0.640	0.846	0.718

It is evident from these findings that the industrial growth of the Scheduled Castes is responding fairly well to the industrial and economic growth of the state as a whole.

Industrial Development: As already mentioned, the percentage of non-agricultural occupations has been taken as an index of industrialization on the assumption that a higher percentage of these occupations represents a greater proportion of occupations in the modern industrial sector. But in 1961 and earlier, the growth of the modern industrial sector as represented by industries other than the household industry, was minimal, and a relatively large proportion of the industries belonged to the household sector in which the Scheduled Castes were better represented. Accordingly, the index score on equality of industrialization (IEI) for the Scheduled Castes was quite high in 1961. It was 70 for the country as a whole (Table 4.10, column 5) compared with the IEE and IEU scores of 39 and 56 respectively during the same year. This higher score should not be taken to mean that the Scheduled Castes were better represented in industrial development in 1961.

The overall IEI score actually came down to 63 in 1971 (Table 4.11, column 5) and rose slightly to 66 in 1981 (Table 4.12 column 5). The IEI score in 1981 compares more evenly with the IEE and IEU scores in the same year, which were 55 and 64 respectively.

The industrial development (IEI) of the Scheduled Castes is also highly disparate across the states. Orissa had the highest score in 1961 and 1971, but it was overtaken by Gujarat in 1981 when the IEI score had begun to represent modernization. The lowest rank on IEI score went to Andhra Pradesh in 1961 and to Tamil Nadu in 1971; in 1981 Tamil Nadu and Andhra Pradesh tied for the last rank. The ranges in 1961, 1971 and 1981 were 100, 63 and 66 respectively. If we ignore the situation of 1961, it would appear that the inter-regional inequality between the states with the highest and the lowest industrial development has widened.

The correlation between industrial development of the Scheduled Castes (IEI score) and their industrial growth (per cent non-agricultural workers) was rather low in 1961, but has improved over the decades; the coefficients of correlation between the two variables in 1961, 1971 and 1981 were 0.406, 0.582 and 0.618 respectively. The correlations are considerably weaker than their counterparts in education and urbanization (seen already), which is understandable in view of the fact that the percentage of non-agricultural occupations is a coarser index of industrialization, especially during the earlier decades.

It is, however, interesting to note that the industrial development of the Scheduled Castes bears a negative correlation with the percentage of non-agricultural workers among the non-Scheduled Castes, which generally represents the regional growth in industrialization. This would mean that regional industrial growth has been inequitable to the Scheduled Castes. But the saving grace lies in the fact that the degree of negative correlation has tended to decline over the decades; the coefficients of correlation between the IEI scores of the Scheduled Castes and the percentage of non-agricultural workers among the non-Scheduled Castes in 1961, 1971 and 1981 are −0.439, −0.345 and −0.189 respectively. On the other hand, the correlation between the IEI score of the Scheduled Castes and the PCDP (economic development) of the state is negligible, the coefficients of correlation between the two variables in 1961, 1971 and 1981 being −0.126, 0.257 and 0.248 respectively. Thus, industrial growth and economic development of the state has not so far directly contributed towards the industrial development of the Scheduled Castes; in fact, in the earlier phases of growth, the Scheduled Castes had actually come down in their relative industrial status in those states which had shown better industrial growth.

An Overview of Modernization and the Development of the Scheduled Castes

Our analysis so far has shown that with regard to every variable of modernization, the patterns of growth and development of the Scheduled Castes follow markedly different kinds of relationships with the overall growth of the region in its economy as well as in the respective variable. It shows that the growth of a region at large also promotes the growth of the Scheduled Castes, but it does not ensure their development (improvement in their relative status). Only in the case of their educational development does regional educational growth show a low to moderate degree of relationship.

The lack of correlation between the development of the Scheduled Castes and the growth of the state in a given variable does not mean that the Scheduled Castes have not benefited from development planning. As a matter of fact, their scores on the indexes of equality have consistently improved over the years (except in the case of the IEI score from 1961–71), although the degree of improvement may not be considered to be adequate. The Scheduled Castes in some states have fared better in their developmental variables. An inter-state comparison of the developmental status of the Scheduled Castes can be made by comparing the rank of a state on the development index score of the Scheduled Castes (rank on the IEE, IEU or IEI score given in column 6) with its rank in the growth of the non-Scheduled Castes (rank in percentage distribution given in column 4) on a given variable presented in Tables 4.1, 4.2 and 4.3 which deal with education, Tables 4.6, 4.7 and 4.8 which deal with urbanization, and Tables 4.10, 4.11 and 4.12 which deal with industrialization. The comparison would indicate by how many steps the rank on the development of the Scheduled Castes is higher (+), lower (−) or equal (0) to the rank on the growth of the non-Scheduled Castes. Table 4.13 gives the figures which represent the differences in the ranks between the two variables in respect of education, urbanization and indus-trialization at the three points of time in each case.

Table 4.13 gives a summary of the foregoing analysis of the regional pattern of the development of the Scheduled Castes from 1961 to 1981. A careful examination of the table reveals some remarkable features. First, it can be seen that, with a few exceptions, the scores in any state (indicating the differences between the ranks of the two variables considered) are either all or mostly positive, or all or mostly negative. Also, the dimensions of the scores in a state are, by and large, of the same order. Such a pattern would imply that, in a given state, the development of the Scheduled Castes in the different variables of modernization is of a similar order. In other words, the development in the different variables is mutually reinforcing. It also shows that relative devel-opment in any variable over the years has remained stable.

The states worth noting which do not fully feature in this pattern are Bihar, Karnataka and Kerala. Bihar shows an unfavourable situation as regards education but distinctly favourable develop-mental situation with regard to urbanization and industrialization. Karnataka shows a highly unfavourable situation with regard to education and nearly normal situations with regard to the other two variables (if we ignore the aberrant case of industrialization in 1961). Kerala reveals a highly unfavourable situation with respect to industrialization as compared with the other two variables.

Table 4.13

Number of Positions by which the Index of Equality Score of the Scheduled Castes is Ranked in Relation to the Percentage Distribution of the Non-Scheduled Castes in a Given Variable by States and Variables of Modernization (1961, 1971 and 1981)

State	Education			Urbanization			Industrialization		
	1961	1971	1981	1961	1971	1981	1961	1971	1981
(Reference to table)	4.1	4.2	4.3	4.6	4.7	4.8	4.10	4.11	4.12
	(1)	(2)	(3)	(4)	(5)	(6)	(7)	(8)	(9)
Andhra Pradesh	0	−3	+3	−1	−1	−3	−8	−4	−4
Bihar	−2	−1	−1	+5	+6	+6	+3	+5	+4
Gujarat	+3	+5	+5	+3	+3	+2	+3	+6	+5
Haryana	NA	−1	−3	NA	−3	+1	NA	+2	0
Karnataka	−5	−5	−5	+1	0	0	+9	−1	0
Kerala	−2	−1	−1	0	+2	+3	−7	−9	−8
Madhya Pradesh	+7	+7	+8	+6	+6	+7	+6	+7	+11
Maharashtra	+3	0	0	0	0	0	−2	0	+4
Orissa	+4	+5	+4	+7	+9	+9	+8	+11	+6
Punjab	−5	−7	−6	−7	−5	−7	+2	−3	−4
Rajasthan	+5	+6	+6	+5	+7	+5	+6	+7	+6
Tamil Nadu	−4	−4	−4	−9	−11	−11	−8	−11	−9
Uttar Pradesh	0	+1	−1	0	−1	−2	−2	0	0
West Bengal	−4	−2	−3	−10	−11	−9	−10	−10	−10

Note: + denotes higher than; − denotes lower than; 0 denotes equal to.
Figures in columns 1–9 are based on Tables 4.1–4.12 respectively.

However, even in these states where consistency is lacking between the variables, the pattern is stable within each variable over the years.

Thus, barring a few exceptions, the pattern of scores in Table 4.13 provides evidence of the stable character of the regional disparities in the development of the Scheduled Castes, which has persisted over the years despite development planning.

A second remarkable feature of the distribution of scores in Table 4.13 is that most of the states can be neatly divided into two categories, the first with a favourable developmental status for the Scheduled Castes and the second with an unfavourable status. The states of Gujarat, Madhya Pradesh, Orissa and Rajasthan clearly fall into the first category, and Punjab, Tamil Nadu, West Bengal and Andhra Pradesh belong to the second category. Among the other states, Maharashtra can be included in the first category.

considering the fact that the ranks on the developmental variables of the Scheduled Castes are equal to or even better than the ranks on the growth of the non-Scheduled Castes, which themselves are relatively high. By a similar logic Uttar Pradesh may be included in the second category. In Uttar Pradesh the ranks on the growth of the non-Scheduled Castes are very low (coming within the last four ranks), and the ranks on the developmental variables of the Scheduled Castes are even lower. What is important to note about these two categories of states is that the states falling in any one of the categories are not relatively more homogeneous in economic development as compared to the states falling in the other category. Therefore, economic development as such does not account for the particular developmental status of the Scheduled Castes in a given state.

The pattern of regional inequalities in development has remained, by and large, constant over the two decades from 1961 to 1981. This also emphasizes the fact that development planning has not been able to bring about any transformation of the existing inequalitarian system.

Social-Structural Factors

Since the broader regional growth, for the most part, does not influence the regional variation in the development of the Scheduled Castes, it stands to reason to assume that the latter variable is strongly influenced by the structural forces which have pegged the Scheduled Castes to the bottom of the social hierarchy for centuries together. Our analysis of social mobility in Chapter 2 has made it clear that there has been very little upward mobility experienced by the people of the lower strata. Much of whatever little mobility there has been is due to social capillarity or certain fortuitous circumstances.

We may briefly consider some of the fortuitous circumstances related to the social structure which provide the Scheduled Castes with a special opportunity of mobility. As already pointed out, the society (social structure) and the economy (occupational structure) intersect in occupational prestige. The positions and prestige which individuals enjoy in the social structure are basically derived from the prestige of occupations which they follow in the economic system.

In a given economic stystem, occupations of different prestige gradations are found in certain proportions which remain more or less constant in a stagnant economy; and there is a correspondence between the gradations of occupations in the economic system and the gradations in the social structure. When there is economic development, the relative proportions of the occupational prestige gradations undergo a change, usually the proportions of higher gradations expanding at the expense of those of the lower gradations. In that event, as illustrated by the case of mobility in Rayya (Sethi, 1982), some of the persons from the lower rungs of the social structure get a chance for upward mobility if only because the persons in the higher rungs cannot fully exhaust the expanding opportunities. If, in addition, the proportion of persons in the lower rungs of the social structure is smaller, the greater is their chance of upward mobility.

Secondly, since, in general, groups in the higher rungs of the social structure benefit more than those in the lower rungs, if the Scheduled Castes (who normally occupy the lowest rung) happen to occupy a higher rung in the socio-economic hierarchy, they would have a better chance of upward mobility.

As will be shown presently, the Scheduled Tribes, wherever present (especially in the larger states), occupy an even lower position than the Scheduled Castes in the economic hierarchy of the states. In such a setting the Scheduled Castes have a better opportunity for social mobility than they would have had if they were to occupy the bottom rung of the economic hierarchy in the absence of the Scheduled Tribes.

The fore-mentioned two structural contexts of social mobility for the Scheduled Castes in the face of industrial and economic growth give rise to two important hypotheses which are capable of being tested with census data. One, the lower the population percentage of Scheduled Castes in a state, the better their chances of mobility. Secondly, the higher the population percentage of Scheduled Tribes in a state, the better the chances of mobility for the Scheduled Castes. These hypotheses, as already explained, refer to the structural aspects of change. Since the variation in the development of the Scheduled Castes cannot be explained by the growth of the region, we shall now see whether it can be explained by these hypotheses derived from the social-structural dynamics.

Population and Development
of the Scheduled Castes

It has already been illustrated that the growth of the Scheduled Castes in all the variables of modernization shows a high to very high degree of correlation with the growth of the region in the respective variables as well as in its economy. Therefore, we do not expect any high degree of relationship between the growth in any one of these variables and the structural dimensions (such as, the population percentage of the Scheduled Castes). The details are given in Table 4.14 only for 1981 to serve as illustration. Accordingly, we find the following low degrees of correlation coefficients between the percentage of Scheduled Caste population and the relevant variables:

Variables Correlated with Population Percentage of the Scheduled Castes	Coefficients of Correlation		
	1961	1971	1981
Percentage of literacy among the SCs	−0.418	−0.365	−0.292
Percentage of urban residents among the SCs	−0.401	−0.360	−0.187
Percentage of non-agricultural workers among the total SC workers	0.016	−0.266	−0.252

The relationship between the percentage of Scheduled Castes in the population of a state with the growth in each of the variables of modernization is of a low to negligible degree in every case, as expected. It is also negative as predicted by the hypothesis. In the case of literacy and urbanization, the coefficients of correlation have declined from 1961 to 1981. Thus, the constraint exerted by the size of their population upon the growth of the Scheduled Castes in these variables is disappearing.

On the other hand, the relationship of the percentage of the Scheduled Caste population with the scores on the indexes of development of the Scheduled Castes is found to be much stronger. The percentages of the Scheduled Caste population along with its ranks as well as the ranks according to scores on the IEE, IEU and IEI, in the various states are shown in Table 4.14 which refers to the census data of 1981. The patterns for 1971 and 1961 are also

Table 4.14

Ranks of the Scheduled Castes on Indices of Development Compared with Ranks according to the Percentage Distribution of their Population in the Larger States (1981)

State	SC Population		Ranks on Indices of Equality		
	%	Rank	IEE	IEU	IEI
Andhra Pradesh	14.87	8	7	10	13
Bihar	14.51	10	14	7	10
Gujarat	7.15	13	1	1	1
Haryana	19.00	4	11	7	5
Karnataka	15.07	7	12	6	8
Kerala	10.02	12	2	9	9
Madhya Pradesh	14.10	11	4	3	2
Maharashtra	7.14	14	3	2	3
Orissa	14.66	9	5	5	6
Punjab	26.87	1	10	11	7
Rajasthan	17.04	6	8	4	4
Tamil Nadu	18.35	5	6	12	13
Uttar Pradesh	21.16	3	12	13	11
West Bengal	21.99	2	8	14	12

Source: *Census of India*, 1981, Primary Census Abstract, General Population, and Scheduled Castes; and Tables 4.3, 4.8 and 4.12 in this book.

similar (not shown in the table). The coefficients of correlation between the percentage of the Scheduled Caste population and each of the variables of development are as follows:

Developmental Variables Correlated with Percentage of SC Population	Coefficients of Correlation		
	1961	1971	1981
IEE	−0.571	−0.486	−0.640
IEU	−0.753	−0.745	−0.751
IEI	−0.121	−0.052	−0.488

The correlation coefficients are all negative, indicating the inhibiting effect of the percentage of the Scheduled Caste population on their development. But they are sufficiently strong so as to confirm our hypothesis only in the case of the IEE and IEU. In this case, the coefficients have also become stronger from 1961 to 1981. Therefore, regarding the educational and urban development of the Scheduled Castes, the strong negative influence of the percentage of their population may explain, to some extent, the lack of influence of the overall growth of the region in the respective variables as well as in its economy.

The coefficient of correlation between the percentage of the Scheduled Caste population and their IEI is nil or negligible in 1961 and 1971, and moderate in 1981. But it is significant that, although smaller, the degree of correlation has increased substantially in 1981. It may be recalled that the percentage of non-agricultural occupations was a poor index of industrialization in the past as the share of manufacturing occupations in the organized sector was too small; as its proportion has become greater as of 1981, this relationship has become relatively stronger.

Population of the Scheduled Tribes and the Development of the Scheduled Castes

It has been hypothesized that if the larger percentage of the Scheduled Caste population in the total serves as an encumberance to their development, their association with the larger population of the Scheduled Tribes in a state tends to facilitate their development. As already clarified, when a society is rigidly stratified, the population percentage of different strata tends to acquire structural characteristics. The Scheduled Castes gain a structural advantage if the Scheduled Tribes occupy a lower position than their own in the variables of modernization.

That the Scheduled Tribes indeed occupy lower levels on the variables of modernization as compared with the Scheduled Castes is evident from the data presented in Table 4.15. In 1981, in the country as a whole, the Scheduled Tribes were about three-quarters as developed in education as the Scheduled Castes; in urbanization and in industrialization their relative growth was to the tune of about two-fifths and half, respectively. So also, with some exceptions, the Scheduled Tribes in any state were very much behind the Scheduled Castes in every variable. The striking exceptions are Bihar as regards education and industrialization, and Uttar Pradesh as regards education. In Bihar, the Scheduled Tribes have stolen a march over the Scheduled Castes in education because of the work of the Christian missionaries among the Tribes.

Table 4.15

Distribution of Scheduled Tribes in the Larger States according to their Population Percentage in the Total and their IEE, IEU and IEI Scores Relative to the Scheduled Castes (1981)

State	Population (%)	Index Scores on Equality Relative to SCs		
		Education	Urbanization	Industrialization
Andhra Pradesh	5.93	44	41	91
Bihar	8.31	163	73	101
Gujarat	14.22	53	22	33
Haryana	—	—	—	—
Karnataka	4.91	98	59	70
Kerala	1.03	57	16	55
Madhya Pradesh	22.97	56	20	32
Maharashtra	9.19	63	33	41
Orissa	22.43	62	49	49
Punjab	—	—	—	—
Rajasthan	12.21	73	21	40
Tamil Nadu	1.07	69	48	99
Uttar Pradesh	0.21	137	45	81
West Bengal	5.63	54	30	74
India	7.76	76	39	51

Source: *Census of India*, 1981, Primary Census Abstract, Scheduled Castes, and Scheduled Tribes.

Thus the conditions for the population percentage of the Scheduled Tribes to act as a structural factor in the development of the Scheduled Castes exist. We should, therefore, see to what extent the percentage of the population of the Scheduled Tribes is positively related with the development of the Scheduled Castes in the variables of modernization.

Developmental Variables of SCs Correlated with the Population Percentage of STs in the State	*Coefficients of Correlation*		
	1961	*1971*	*1981*
IEE	0.309	0.459	0.501
IEU	0.563	0.719	0.659
IEI	0.682	0.510	0.568

The coefficients of correlation are all positive in the relationship between each of the developmental variables of Scheduled Castes and the percentage of the population of the Scheduled Tribes, unlike their relationship with the percentage of population of the Scheduled Castes where the corresponding coefficients are all negative. It is, therefore, evident that in structural terms it is advantageous to the Scheduled Castes to have the Scheduled Tribes living in their states in larger proportions for, in that case, the bottom layers in the modernization variables would be filled by the latter, which improves the mobility chances of the former.

Except in the case of IEE in 1961, the coefficients of correlation are of a moderate to high degree. The coefficients are of a relatively higher degree in the case of the IEU, especially in 1971 and 1981. The reason why the coefficient of correlation is relatively stronger when the percentage of the population of the Scheduled Tribes is correlated with the IEU and relatively weaker when it is correlated with the IEE becomes obvious when we consider the fact that the growth of the Scheduled Tribes in relation to the Scheduled Castes is the least in the case of urbanization and the most in the case of education (Table 4.15). This would also mean that the presence of the Scheduled Tribes in a larger proportion in a state is not necessarily beneficial to the development of the Scheduled Castes if the former are equally or even more advanced than the latter in a given variable.

When we consider the fact that both the percentage of the Scheduled Caste population and of the Scheduled Tribe population in a state are correlated with the development of the Scheduled Castes, the influence of the structural dimensions on the development of the Scheduled Castes would add up to a substantial measure. This substantial degree of influence of the structural factors acts as a countervailing force to neutralize the influence of the overall growth of the region upon the development of the Scheduled Castes in a given variable. On the other hand, the structural factors (the population of Scheduled Castes and Scheduled Tribes) have very little influence on the growth of the Scheduled Castes in a given variable; that is why whereas the development of the Scheduled Castes in a given variable is not influenced by the overall growth of the region in that variable, their growth in that variable is highly related to regional growth.

Mutual Influence among
the Developmental Variables

Another aspect of the development of Scheduled Castes in a given variable is the influence which the development in the other variables exerts on it. The mutual influence of the developmental variables is shown below:

Pairs of Variables Correlated	Coefficients of Correlation		
	1961	1971	1981
IEE and IEU	0.434	0.314	0.448
IEE and IEI	0.374	0.425	0.421
IEU and IEI	0.472	0.710	0.878

It may be pointed out that the correlations between educational (IEE) and industrial development (IEI), and between educational and urban development (IEU) are of a low degree in all the years. But the correlation between urban and industrial development is quite high; it has risen continually from 1961 to 1981 when it was of a very high degree. One of the inferences which can be drawn is that since the urban and industrial development of the Scheduled Castes is not based very much on their educational development, in the urban areas the Scheduled Castes fill non-agricultural occupations at the lower levels of skill.

Supplementary Evidence in
Educational Development

In the modernization of the Scheduled Castes, the most attention has been paid to improving their educational background. Efforts are also being made to monitor the results achieved in this respect. Accordingly, the Ministry of Education has been collecting information on the enrolment of students of the major sections of the population—Scheduled Castes, Scheduled Tribes and Other Backward Communities—at various educational levels and on other related aspects. Some of this information has been further analysed by interested scholars (such as, Nautiyal and Sharma, 1978). It is interesting to see how enrolment in educational institutions is reflected in the census data on the educational development of the Scheduled Castes.

The developmental index, coefficient of equality (CE), computed from the enrolment data differs slightly from the index of equality on education (IEE) discussed already:

$$\text{Coefficient of equality} = \frac{\text{Percentage of enrolment of SCs to the total enrolment}}{\text{Percentage of the population of the SCs to the total population}} \times 100$$

The coefficients of equality (CE) for the Scheduled Castes in enrolment at the various school levels (including the High and Higher Secondary levels) in the larger states of India in 1960–61, 1970–71 and 1980–81 are given in Table 4.16. As one can see from the table, even in 1981 the Scheduled Castes lagged behind the general population in their school enrolment. But their rate of enrolment in relative terms had picked up sharply from 1970–71 to 1980–81 when the CE scores for the country as a whole rose from 67 to 89, whereas from 1960–61 to 1970–71 they increased merely from 65 to 67.

The ranks of the states on the CE scores have remained relatively stable, the coefficients of correlation between the ranks in 1960–61 and 1970–71 and between 1970–71 and 1980–81 being 0.813 and 0.759. Only three states show a substantial change in their ranks from 1960–61 to 1970–71; Bihar has declined in rank from 7 to 11, Orissa has improved from 11 to 6 and West Bengal has declined from 6 to 10. There are, however, many more states which have undergone a substantial change in their ranks from 1970–71 to 1980–81. Those which deserve special mention are Andhra Pradesh (improvement by 3 ranks), Haryana (improvement by 4 ranks), Karnataka (decline by 4 ranks), Punjab (improvement by 6 ranks), and West Bengal (decline by 4 ranks). Bihar and West Bengal are especially worth noting for their continual decline in rank.

The ranks of the states on the CE scores on enrolment of the Scheduled Castes are to some extent correlated with their ranks on the IEE scores. The coefficient of correlation, which was rather small (0.425) in 1960–61, rose substantially in strength in 1970–71 (0.730) and 1980–81 (0.661). There are also indications that the

Table 4.16

Coefficient of Equality for the Scheduled Castes in Enrolment at Various School
Levels in the Larger States (1960–61, 1970–71 and 1980–81)

State	1960–61		1970–71		1980–81	
	Score	Rank	Score	Rank	Score	Rank
Andhra Pradesh	77	4	77	5	119	2
Bihar	57	7	52	11	67	13
Gujarat	89	3	93	3	115	3
Haryana*	NA	—	50	14	75	10
Karnataka	56	8	66	7	74	11
Kerala	115	2	106	2	114	4
Madhya Pradesh	52	10	58	8	86	9
Maharashtra	172	1	122	1	206	1
Orissa	51	11	68	6	89	7
Punjab*	44	12	51	12	92	6
Rajasthan	21	13	51	12	74	11
Tamil Nadu	74	5	89	4	103	5
Uttar Pradesh	56	8	58	8	88	8
West Bengal	73	6	55	10	62	14
India	65		67		89	

Source: K.C. Nautiyal and Y.D. Sharma, *Equalization of Educational Opportunities for Scheduled Castes and Scheduled Tribes*, New Delhi, NCERT,
1978; Ministry of Education, Government of India, *State-wise Information
on Education of Scheduled Castes and Scheduled Tribes*, New Delhi, 1985.
* Punjab includes Haryana in 1961.

changes in the ranks of the states on the CE scores on enrolments
at different points of time are linked with the changes in their
ranks according to the IEE scores.

    As in the case of the IEE scores, there is wide variation in the
CE scores on the enrolment of the Scheduled Castes in the different
states. The variation in the CE scores is also negatively correlated
with the percentage of the Scheduled Caste population. There is,
however, a tendency for the structural constraint to weaken since
the coefficients of correlation between the rank on the CE scores
and that on the percentage of the Scheduled Caste population has
declined from -0.707 to -0.470 from 1971 to 1981. In this respect,
the variation in the CE scores resembles that in the IEE scores
but, unlike the IEE scores, the CE scores on enrolment are not
correlated with the percentage of the Scheduled Caste population.

Even in the case of the IEE scores, it was noticed that the influence of structural factors (especially those represented by the population of the Scheduled Tribes) was less marked than in the case of the IEU scores. In the case of educational development, the overall development of the state also plays a significant role. In the case of the CE scores on the enrolment of the Scheduled Castes also, such a trend is noticeable; whereas the consistently high levels of CE scores in the economically advanced states of Maharashtra and Gujarat are also due to the relatively small percentage of Scheduled Caste population in these states, the improvement in ranks on the CE scores in Punjab and Haryana from 1970–71 to 1980–81 (despite their high Scheduled Caste population) can be attributed to their economic development. However, the coefficient of correlation between the rank on the CE scores and the rank on the per capita domestic product in 1981 was of a small degree (0.313).

On the whole, the patterns of educational development of the Scheduled Castes, as potrayed by the IEE scores and by the CE scores, correspond with each other.

A point which needs to be emphasized in viewing the development of the Scheduled Castes (which also holds good in the development of the Scheduled Tribes), is that the variables of modernization we have considered—such as, literacy, urbanization and the percentage of non-agricultural occupations—at best can give us a view of their development from the bottom. Even when the Scheduled Castes have attained parity with the rest of the population in these variables, they might be lagging behind in variables at a higher level of modernization. For example, even when the IEE score of the Scheduled Castes in literacy is 100, their IEE scores on higher education can be much lower. Such a discrepancy can be easily noticed in the pattern of enrolment of the Scheduled Castes in educational institutions at different levels.

A comparison of Table 4.16 and Table 4.17 (which shows the CE scores on enrolment of the Scheduled Castes in the High/Higher Secondary schools [classes IX-XII]) reveals that as we go up the educational ladder, the CE scores of a state become much lower. With the odd exception (as in the case of Uttar Pradesh in 1981, which is perhaps due to factual inaccuracy), the CE score at the High/Higher Secondary school enrolment is lower than in the case of enrolment in all the schools in every state and at every point of time. It is obvious that as one advances in the educational ladder, the drop-out rates among the Scheduled Caste students is much higher than among the non-Scheduled Caste students in every state and at every point of time. But, over the years, this difference has tended to decline, which augurs well for the educational development of the Scheduled Castes.

Table 4.17
Coefficient of Equality for the Scheduled Castes in Enrolment at the High/Higher Secondary School Level in the Larger States (1960–61, 1970–71 and 1980–81)

State	1960–61		1970–71		1980–81	
	Score	Rank	Score	Rank	Score	Rank
Andhra Pradesh	54	3	62	5	120	2
Bihar	37	8	33	11	44	13
Gujarat	49	4	70	3	92	5
Haryana*	NA	—	45	7	54	9
Karnataka	39	7	52	6	75	6
Kerala	88	2	91	2	98	4
Madhya Pradesh	23	11	42	9	72	8
Maharashtra	125	1	107	1	174	1
Orissa	17	12	29	13	53	11
Punjab*	36	9	43	8	54	9
Rajasthan	14	13	31	12	50	12
Tamil Nadu	40	5	66	4	74	7
Uttar Pradesh	40	5	40	10	110	3
West Bengal	25	10	27	14	39	14
India	41		48		77	

Source: K.C. Nautiyal and Y.D. Sharma, *Equalization of Educational Oppor-tunities for Scheduled Castes and Scheduled Tribes*, New Delhi, NCERT, 1978; Ministry of Education, Government of India, *State-wise Information on Education of Scheduled Castes and Scheduled Tribes*, New Delhi, 1985.
   * Punjab includes Haryana in 1960–61.

Influence of Regional Growth and Structural Factors on the Scheduled Castes in Each State

So far, we have analysed the pattern of growth and development of the Scheduled Castes in the country as a whole with the larger states as units. Let us now examine the development of each state separately in relation to the other states in order to find out if the logic of our findings for the country as a whole is reflected in the developmental situation in each state. If there is no interference of structural factors, the development of the Scheduled Castes should agree with the growth of the non-Scheduled Caste population in a given variable. If it does not agree, the discrepancy should be in agreement with structural factors.

Tables 4.18, 4.19 and 4.20 provide a synoptic view of the variables of development of the Scheduled Castes and their major correlates of regional growth and structural factors in 1961, 1971 and 1981 respectively. The state-wise distribution of each variable is converted into its rank. The first set (columns 1–3) refers to regional growth as indicated by the percentage of non-Scheduled Castes in education (literacy), urbanization and industrialization (non-agricultural workers). The second set refers to the three developmental variables of the Scheduled Castes, namely, scores on the IEE, IEU and IEI. The third set consists of the structural variables as represented by the population percentage of the Scheduled Castes and Scheduled Tribes.

Assuming that the growth of the region would lead to the development of the Scheduled Castes, there should be a consistency between the rank of the corresponding variables in set I and the IEE in set II. If the two ranks are not consistent with each other, the discrepancy, according to our findings discussed above, should be explained by the factors in set III. A satisfactory explanation would be along the following lines. If the rank on the IEE of a state is inferior (larger in number) to its rank on education (column 1), it would be due to either one or both of the two reasons: (i) the rank of the state on its percentage of Scheduled Caste population is relatively higher (smaller in number), and (ii) its rank on its percentage of the Scheduled Tribe population is relatively lower (larger in number); i.e., (a) the Scheduled Castes are over-represented, and (b) the Scheduled Tribes are under-represented.

There can be, of course, exceptions to this explanation. For example, as already pointed out, the Scheduled Tribe population acts as a positive factor in the development of the Scheduled Castes in a given variable, only if the former is less advanced than the latter in that variable, and there are some exceptions to this general condition (see Table 4.15).

Table 4.18

Developmental Variables of the Scheduled Castes, the Corresponding Variables of Regional Growth and the Population Percentage of the Scheduled Castes and Scheduled Tribes according to their Ranks in the Larger States of India (1961)

State	Percentage of Non-SC Population (I)			Development of SCs (II)			Population Percentage (III)	
	Education (1)	Urbanization (2)	Industrialization (3)	IEE (4)	IEU (5)	IEI (6)	SC (7)	ST (8)
Andhra Pradesh	9	7	5	9	8	13	8	8
Bihar	11	12	10	13	7	7	7	5
Gujarat	4	4	6	1	1	3	12	3
Karnataka	7	6	13	12	5	4	9	10
Kerala	1	9	1	3	9	8	11	9
Madhya Pradesh	12	10	12	5	4	6	10	2
Maharashtra	5	2	7	2	2	9	13	6
Orissa	8	13	9	4	6	1	6	1
Punjab	6	5	4	11	12	2	2	—
Rajasthan	13	8	11	8	3	5	5	4
Tamil Nadu	2	1	3	6	10	11	4	11
Uttar Pradesh	10	11	8	10	11	10	1	—
West Bengal	3	3	2	7	13	12	3	7

Source: *Census of India*, 1961, Special Tables for Scheduled Castes, and for Scheduled Tribes; also, Tables 4.1, 4.6 and 4.10 in this book.

Table 4.19

Developmental Variables of the Scheduled Castes, the Corresponding Variables of Regional Growth and the Population Percentage of the Scheduled Castes and Scheduled Tribes according to their Ranks in the Larger States of India (1971)

State	Percentage of Non-SC Population (I)			Development of SCs (II)			Population Percentage (III)	
	Education (1)	Urbanization (2)	Industrialization (3)	IEE (4)	IEU (5)	IEI (6)	SC (7)	ST (8)
Andhra Pradesh	10	7	9	13	8	13	9	8
Bihar	13	13	14	14	7	9	8	5
Gujarat	6	4	3	1	1	2	13	3
Haryana	8	8	7	9	11	4	4	—
Karnataka	7	6	8	12	6	8	10	10
Kerala	1	11	1	2	9	10	12	9
Madhya Pradesh	12	10	12	5	4	6	11	2
Maharashtra	3	2	5	3	2	5	14	6
Orissa	9	14	11	4	5	1	7	1
Punjab	4	5	6	11	10	7	1	—
Rajasthan	14	9	10	8	2	3	6	4
Tamil Nadu	2	1	2	6	12	14	5	11
Uttar Pradesh	11	12	13	10	13	11	2	12
West Bengal	5	3	4	7	14	12	3	7

Source: *Census of India*, 1971, Special Tables for Scheduled Castes, and for Scheduled Tribes; and Tables 4.2, 4.7 and 4.11 in this book.

Table 4.20

Developmental Variables of the Scheduled Castes, the Corresponding Variables of Regional Growth and the Population Percentage of the Scheduled Castes and Scheduled Tribes according to their Ranks in the Larger States of India (1981)

State	Percentage of Non-SC Population (I)			Development of SCs (II)			Population Percentage (III)	
	Education (1)	Urbanization (2)	Industrialization (3)	IEE (4)	IEU (5)	IEI (6)	SC (7)	ST (8)
Andhra Pradesh	10	7	9	7	10	13	8	7
Bihar	13	13	14	14	7	10	10	6
Gujarat	6	3	6	1	1	1	13	3
Haryana	8	8	5	11	7	5	4	—
Karnataka	7	6	8	12	6	8	7	9
Kerala	1	12	1	2	9	9	12	11
Madhya Pradesh	12	10	13	4	3	2	11	1
Maharashtra	3	2	7	3	2	3	14	5
Orissa	9	14	12	5	5	6	9	2
Punjab	4	4	3	10	11	7	1	—
Rajasthan	14	9	10	8	4	4	6	4
Tamil Nadu	2	1	4	6	12	13	5	10
Uttar Pradesh	11	11	11	12	13	11	3	12
West Bengal	5	5	2	8	14	12	2	8

Source: *Census of India*, 1981, Primary Census Abstract, Scheduled Castes, and for Scheduled Tribes; and Tables 4.3, 4.8 and 4.12 in this book.

We shall now evaluate the pattern of ranks in the different sets (I, II and III) of variables in each state with the help of the above hypothesis. It should be borne in mind that Table 4.18 deals with 13 states (as against 14 states in Tables 4.19 and 4.20). Because of this and other minor discrepancies, when comparing the ranks on any two variables, a difference of one rank may be ignored.

In the case of Andhra Pradesh, we find that the ranks of the state on the variables of the growth of the non-Scheduled Castes (set I, columns 1, 2 and 3), and the structural variables (set III, columns 7 and 8) have remained more or less stable over the years (Tables 4.18, 4.19 and 4.20). Among the developmental variables, whereas industrial development of the Scheduled Castes (IEI) has remained constant throughout the period under reference, urban development (IEU) has declined from 1971 to 1981; although educational development (IEE) declined from 1961 to 1971, it has shown a marked improvement from 1971 to 1981, which also agrees with the data on enrolment (Table 4.16).

A significant event that has taken place during the period under reference (which may have a bearing on the remarkable change in the development of the Scheduled Castes in Andhra Pradesh) is the sharp erosion in the percentage of Christians. An analysis of the Scheduled Caste and Christian population in the various districts of the state shows that there is a high degree of correlation between the decrease in the Christian population and an increase in the Scheduled Caste population of a district. Our enquiries with persons with local knowledge reveal that the reversion of Christians to their Scheduled Caste status has taken place mostly in the rural areas. Further, if the Christian recruits to the Scheduled Castes happen to be better educated (as the Christian converts usually are in comparison to their unconverted counterparts), the reversion of a substantial section of the Christian converts to their original caste status would account for an improvement in the educational development of the Scheduled Castes and the deterioration in their urban development. But this peculiar situation demands further study.

When the ranks on the developmental variables are compared with those on the corresponding variables of the growth of the non-Scheduled Castes, the rank in industrial development of the Scheduled Castes (column 6) is consistently lower than the rank on the industrial growth of the non-Scheduled Castes (column 3).

Since the population percentage of both the Scheduled Castes and Scheduledl Tribes in Andhra Pradesh is of moderate levels, this aberration cannot be explained by structural factors. But the ranks on the other variables do not contradict our reasoning.

In Bihar, the developmental pattern (columns 4, 5 and 6) is fairly stable over time except that the rank on industrial development has consistently declined from 7 in 1961 to 10 in 1981. On the whole, the rank on urban development is higher than the ranks on the other two variables. The lowest rank on educational development of the Scheduled Castes in Bihar more or less corresponds with the ranks on the educational growth of the non-Scheduled Castes in that state. Their decline in this respect from 1961 also agrees with their enrolment trend. But their relatively better standing on the other two developmental variables can be attributed to Bihar's relatively higher rank in Scheduled Tribes. But the Scheduled Tribes in this state are relatively more advanced in education and hence the relatively lower standing of the Scheduled Castes on educational development. The Scheduled Tribes are also forging ahead in industrialization, which accounts for the continually declining rank of the Scheduled Castes on industrial development. However, the larger population of the Scheduled Tribes is advantageous to the urban development of the Scheduled Castes inasmuch as the former are far less urbanized than the latter. Accordingly, the Scheduled Castes show a much higher rank in urban development as compared with the rank of the state in regional urbanization (col.2). Thus the structural factors more or less account for the discrepancies between the development of the Scheduled Castes and regional growth in the respective variables.

Gujarat leads in the development of the Scheduled Castes in all the variables in 1981. But in 1961 and 1971 its rank on the IEI was lower (being 3 and 2 respectively). In all the years the ranks on the developmental variables have been consistently higher than the ranks on the growth of the non-Scheduled Castes. The relative advantage enjoyed by the Scheduled Castes in Gujarat can be attributed almost entirely to the structural factors as Gujarat has a very low rank on the percentage of Scheduled Caste population and very high rank on the Scheduled Tribe population, both conditions contributing to the better development of the Scheduled Castes.

Haryana was a part of Punjab state in 1961. From 1971 to 1981 the development of the Scheduled Castes in Haryana has shown a decline in the rank on educational development, a marked increase in the rank on urban development and an almost stationary rank on industrial development. When we compare the development of the Scheduled Castes with regional growth—namely, the ranks of the non-Scheduled Castes (columns 1, 2 and 3)—we find that in 1971 educational and urban development are at lower levels and in 1981 only educational development is falling behind regional growth. Haryana's rapid economic development has helped the Scheduled Castes to develop relatively better in the IEU and IEI. But its relative backwardness in educational development is in agreement with its relatively large percentage of the Scheduled Caste population. The case of Haryana illustrates the fact that structural forces do yield to some drastic changes in the economy.

In Karnataka, the ranks on the variables of development of the Scheduled Castes have declined in 1971 and 1981 as compared with 1961 in respect of urban and industrial development (columns 5 and 6). But they have become consistent with the ranks on regional growth in the respective variables (columns 2 and 3). This situation conforms with the medium rank of Karnataka on the percentage of Scheduled Caste population, which is neither advantageous nor disadvantageous for the development of the Scheduled Castes. The rank on educational development, however, is consistently lower than the rank on regional growth in education, which is not in accordance with structural factors. But, interestingly, the Scheduled Tribes in Karnataka, unlike in most other states, have stolen a march over the Scheduled Castes in education. Perhaps this situation may have retarded the development of the Scheduled Castes commensurate with structural factors.

The structural conditions in Kerala—namely, the low ranks in the population percentage of the Scheduled Castes and Tribes—are supportive of the development of the Scheduled Castes. Accordingly, we do find that the ranks of the state on the educational and urban development of the Scheduled Castes are more or less consistent with its ranks on regional growth in the respective variables. But the rank of the state on the industrial development of the Scheduled Castes is far lower than the rank on the industrialization of the region (column 3). This discrepancy cannot be explained by structural factors.

The development of the Scheduled Castes in Madhya Pradesh is much better than the support available from regional growth in all the variables and in all the years. The advantageous situation of the Scheduled Castes in this case is fully in accord with the structural factors inasmuch as Madhya Pradesh has a low Scheduled Caste population and a very high Scheduled Tribe population. Because of these very favourable structural factors, the development of the Scheduled Castes in Madhya Pradesh has gained further momentum from 1971–81.

In Maharashtra, by and large, the growth of the non-Scheduled Castes in the variables of modernization has been quite high as indicated by the ranks (columns 1, 2 and 3) in all the years. These high ranks have been matched or even surpassed by the ranks of the state on the development of the Scheduled Castes in the respective variables (columns 4, 5 and 6). Such a satisfactory situation in Maharashtra is clearly in agreement with the prevalent structural factors in the state, namely, a very low rank on the percentage of the Scheduled Caste population and a moderately high rank on the percentage of the Scheduled Tribe population.

Orissa, like Gujarat and Madhya Pradesh, is another state where the ranks on the developmental variables of the Scheduled Castes far outweigh the ranks on regional growth in the respective variables in all the years. The contributory factors here also, as in the other two states, are primarily structural ones. Although the rank of Orissa on the percentage of Scheduled Castes is of a medium level, its rank on the percentage of the Scheduled Tribe population is the highest.

Like Orissa, Rajasthan also displays much higher ranks on the development of the Scheduled Castes as compared with the ranks on the regional growth in the respective variables. And it is clear that, as in Rajasthan, it is the relatively high rank on the population of the Scheduled Castes in the state which is responsible for this.

If Orissa has the highest percentage of Scheduled Tribe population, Punjab has the highest percentage of Scheduled Castes. This has the opposite effect of what is produced by the former factor as regards the development of the Scheduled Castes. Accordingly, as one would expect, the ranks on the developmental variables (columns 4, 5 and 6) of the Scheduled Castes in Punjab are far lower than those on the corresponding variables of regional growth (columns 1, 2 and 3), except in the case of the IEI in 1961 when the percentage of non-agricultural occupations was not a satisfactory index of industrialization. In 1971 and 1981, the ranks on the IEI scores became much lower, consistent with the structural factor.

Tamil Nadu and West Bengal display similar patterns of development among the Scheduled Castes. In every year their developmental status is far worse than what is warranted by the levels of growth of the non-Scheduled Castes. And both the states have relatively higher percentages of Scheduled Caste population which seem to have retarded their development. It may also be pointed out that in all the years the difference between the rank of the state on the variable of development of the Scheduled Castes (in set II) and its rank on the corresponding variable of the growth of the non-Scheduled Castes (in set I), especially in urbanization and industrialization, is of a very high degree. It would appear that in these two states, relatively speaking, the development of the Scheduled Castes in urbanization and industrialization is most retarded.

Finally, in Uttar Pradesh we find that the ranks on the variables of both regional growth and the development of the Scheduled Castes are, by and large, consistent with each other and all the ranks are closer to the bottom. Uttar Pradesh has second largest percentage of Scheduled Castes whose effect would be to press down their development. However, the situation in the state is already very low and, therefore, the effect of the structural factor is not visible although it exists very much. By and large, the ranks on the developmental variables of the Scheduled Castes are lower than those on the corresponding variables of regional development.

Thus a detailed evaluation of the developmental patterns of the Scheduled Castes in the various states has revealed that there is rarely a consistency between the overall growth of the state and the development of the Scheduled Castes in any variable of modernization. The discrepancies in most cases agree with the structural factors as represented by the population percentage of the Scheduled Castes and Tribes in the state. Where the structural factors are accentuated (as in the states of Gujarat, Madhya Pradesh, Orissa, Punjab, Rajasthan, Tamil Nadu and West Bengal), there are sharp differences between the overall growth of the state and the development of the Scheduled Castes.

It is conceivable that in bringing about the discrepancy between the overall growth of the state and the development of the Scheduled Castes in any of the variables, the structural factors may be abetted by some other circumstances. One such special feature is evident when one probes into the extreme cases of disjunction, as in the case of Orissa, on the one hand, and Tamil Nadu and West Bengal, on the other. In Orissa, the ranks of the Scheduled Castes on the IEU and IEI (columns 5 and 6 in Tables 4.18, 4.19 and 4.20) are much higher than those of the urbanization and industrialization of the non-Scheduled Castes (columns 2 and 3) respectively, whereas in the case of Tamil Nadu and West Bengal it is the other way round.

As already pointed out, the structural situation of the Scheduled Castes in Orissa (with an over-representation of Scheduled Tribes) is advantageous to their development, whereas that of the Scheduled Castes in Tamil Nadu and West Bengal (with an over-representation of Scheduled Castes) is disadvantageous. But there may be other conditions which may have contributed to this extreme advantage or disadvantage. In this context it may be pointed out that Orissa is the only one among the relatively more backward states, to begin with, which has maintained more than the national average rate of economic growth during the period of planning, whereas Tamil Nadu and West Bengal are the two states among the relatively more developed ones, to begin with, which have fallen below the national average (Dandekar, 1988, p. 50). Such distinctions would indicate that when the structural situation is favourable, the Scheduled Castes are in a position to gain further advantage from a buoyant economy (as in Orissa), and when it is unfavourable, they are likely to suffer a further setback in their development in the face of a depressing economy (as in Tamil Nadu and West Bengal).

It follows from the foregoing evidence that the relatively high developmental status enjoyed by the Scheduled Castes in some states and their relative backwardness in others cannot be attributed to the special efforts or neglect of the states, as the case may be, but are mainly due to fortuitous circumstances of structural factors prevailing in the respective states.

Development Planning and the Growth and Development of the Scheduled Castes

Our major findings so far have been that whereas the growth of the Scheduled Castes in the three major variables of modernization is highly correlated with the regional growth in these variables, there is, by and large, no relationship between the development of the Scheduled Castes in these variables and the regional growth in the respective variables. This is, however, not to ignore the case of education where regional growth has some impact on the educational development of the Scheduled Castes, however small. The peculiar developmental situation of the Scheduled Castes may now be related to the process of development planning in India during the past three decades covering the period 1950–80.

In Chapter 1, the shortcomings of development planning in India from the point of social transformation were referred to. The Indian planners have been overtly concerned with economic growth *per se*. That they have been so driven by certain constraints in the Indian situation is another matter. But the fact is that no serious attempts have been made to set right the glaring inequalities in society, although the need for doing so are well recognized in the plan documents and some special projects in favour of the underprivileged have been promoted.

In general, the strategies of planning may be broadly classified into global and target-group planning. Global planning is aimed at bringing about overall development in the society by first introducing changes in the potentially rich regions and among people who are more receptive to change. It is assumed that the benefits which first accrue to the well-to-do sections would eventually trickle down to the underprivileged masses. The target-group planning strategy, on the other hand, is based on the assumption that certain underprivileged sections of the society are basically deficient in their ability to benefit from opportunities which are open to all. Accordingly, such sections are subjected to exclusive developmental treatment with a view to giving them an added push. For example, if technological improvement is considered important for increasing productivity, in global planning broad conditions are created so that whoever is capable may develop his or her skills, whereas in target-group planning special efforts are made to develop the capabilities and upgrade the skills of the underprivileged.

However, because of the overriding goal of rapid economic growth, the global strategy of planning (which stimulates the overall growth of the economy) has been primarily adopted. Some reforms have also been undertaken by introducing institutional changes but, again, with an eye to economic growth. Of late, some underprivileged sections have been identified and given target-group treatment. But one of the most notable examples of target-group treatment is the provision of protective discrimination in favour of the Scheduled Castes and Scheduled Tribes, especially with regard to their educational growth and development. These sections have, no doubt, also benefited from the various global planning efforts.

The global and target-group planning strategies, however, have different implications for socio-economic change. The strategy of global planning, besides enabling the well-to-do sections to grow first, also induces growth in the lower sections with its trickle-down effect; however, the former would always benefit far more than the latter so that the relative inegalitarian set-up would continue. It is for this reason that we invariably find a high degree of correlation between the growth of the Scheduled Castes (who represent the lower sections) and the growth of the rest of the population (or the non-Scheduled Castes) who represent broadly the higher strata. This kind of relationship can be expected from the fact that development planning in India has been carried out mainly through the strategy of global planning.

On the other hand, the target-group planning strategy (insofar as it gives an edge to the underprivileged sections over the others in the process of growth) amounts to bringing about a transformation in the society inasmuch as it disturbs the old balance of the inegalitarian social order. The reordering of social positions and relations brought about by such a process has been termed development, which is measured by the indexes of equality of the Scheduled Castes in the variables of modernization. Our findings show that with the exception of educational development, there is little or no correlation between the development of the Scheduled Castes and the growth of the rest of the population in the variables of modernization. These findings also agree with the type of development planning followed in India, which has sparingly used the strategy of target-group planning.

The exception of the educational development of the Scheduled Castes—which has a moderate degree of correlation with the educational growth of the non-Scheduled Caste population—also supports our arguments. For, more than in any other sphere, it is in the educational sphere of the Scheduled Castes where target-group planning has been resorted to on a vast scale. Target-group planning in education has provided relatively better opportunities for the Scheduled Castes in every state. However, the absorption of these facilities has not been uniform in all the states as the ability to absorb the new facilities depends upon the already existing level of education of the Scheduled Castes which, among other factors, depends upon the level of education of the general population. Hence, the correlation between the educational level of the non-Scheduled Caste population and the educational development of the Scheduled Castes. The full impact of the level of education of the region upon the educational development of the Scheduled Castes, however, has been checked by structural factors.

It should be pointed out that despite the advantage it has derived from the strategy of planning, the educational development of the Scheduled Castes does not seem to have made its full impact on their industrial and urban development, as the coefficients of correlation of the variable of educational development with each of the latter two variables are of a lower degree as compared with the coefficient of correlation between the latter two.

However, in general, despite the fact that the non-Scheduled Caste population has benefited more than the Scheduled Castes from development planning, it is obvious that the situation of the Scheduled Castes has relatively improved in all the variables of modernization as indicated by the fact that the scores on the indexes of equality have increased from 1971 to 1981 in all the variables. This relative improvement can be explained, to some extent, by the structural factors. When development takes place and opportunities increase, because of the saturation of the higher sections, there would be some room for the lower sections to move upwards. These new opportunities, however, would be limited in volume so that the size of the lower section would determine the level of their gain—the larger the size, the smaller the gain. A further modifying factor is the relative position of the lower sections on the structure of the society—the higher the position, the better are its chances of mobility. This is the interpretation of our findings.

5

Development and the Scheduled Castes: Inter-District Disparities in the States

In the previous chapter we examined the disparities in the development of the Scheduled Castes in the three crucial variables of education, urbanization and industrialization, as compared with the development of the rest of the population, by treating the larger states as units. Our analysis has disclosed certain broad but hitherto unfamiliar trends. The patterns of the absolute, or the percentage growth in the developmental variabes of the Scheduled Castes, differ markedly from those of their relative growth in the respective variables.

The absolute growth of the Scheduled Castes is fairly highly correlated with that of the non-Scheduled Castes, in every variable. In the more developed states, the Scheduled Castes have advanced faster than in the less developed ones. An upshot of this tendency has been the fact that the inequalities between the Scheduled Castes in the most advanced state and the least advanced state have widened over the years.

On the other hand, the relative growth of the Scheduled Castes in the given variables is correlated very little, if at all, with the advancement of the rest of the population. This is because the relative growth is highly related with the social structural situation of the Scheduled Castes, which is represented by the demographic factors (such as, the population percentage of the Scheduled Castes and Tribes in the total).

Our findings would be further confirmed if what is revealed by our analysis of the data for the country as a whole by treating the larger states as units is also replicated in the various states when the districts are taken as units. We shall now examine the situation in each of the fourteen states included in the earlier analysis.

In the state-wise analysis, the districts with entirely urban populations (such as, Greater Bombay in Maharashtra and Calcutta in West Bengal) or entirely rural populations (such as Dangs in Gujarat) have been ignored. It should also be remembered that because of the reorganization of territorial boundaries within the states, the number of districts in a state in 1981 is larger than it was in 1971 in many cases. Therefore, at least some of the discrepancies, if any, between the all-India level and the state level analysis could be attributed to these factors.

Educational Growth and Development

Educational Growth

Just as the percentage of literate Scheduled Castes varies widely from state to state, there is also great deal of variation between districts in each state. The range of variation in each state is quite large, and it has widened from 1971 to 1981 in most states; the medium deviations too have increased (Tables 5.1 and 5.2). An interesting point to be noted in this variation is that the district at the top of the range in 1971 has continued to be either at the top (or within the top two or three positions) in 1981 and the district at the bottom has either continued to be at the bottom or at the bottom second or third position (not shown in the tables). In other words, it is the same districts at the top which are advancing continually whereas at the opposite end it is the same districts at the bottom which are lagging behind. Thus the inequalities in literacy among the Scheduled Castes of different districts have been widening.

However, when we view the overall pattern of inequalities in a relative perspective—which is provided by the coefficient of relative variation $(CRV = \dfrac{\text{median deviation}}{\text{median}} \times 100)$—we find that there is some decline in this pattern over the decade (Tables 5.1 and 5.2, column 7). Therefore, with advancement, the overall inequalities (CRV value) diminish, but the inequality between the extremities (value of the range) increases. Even so, these coefficients of relative variation are quite large and so the reduction in the overall inequalities is not substantial.

Table 5.1

State-wise Educational Growth of the Scheduled Castes (1971)

State	Number of Districts	Percentage of Literacy among SCs in Districts					
		Lowest	Highest	Range	Median	Median Deviation	CRV
	(1)	(2)	(3)	(4)	(5)	(6)	(7)
Andhra Pradesh	21	3.07	19.20	16.13	9.20	4.39	48
Bihar	17	4.78	16.81	12.03	6.45	2.46	38
Gujarat	18	11.70	49.76	38.06	23.64	10.85	46
Haryana	7	7.86	16.87	9.01	16.02	2.72	17
Karnataka	19	6.79	21.20	14.41	12.89	3.19	25
Kerala	10	20.39	54.38	33.99	41.56	8.38	20
Madhya Pradesh	43	2.83	39.93	37.10	10.87	5.43	50
Maharashtra	25	10.22	40.51	30.29	27.42	5.89	21
Orissa	13	9.19	20.54	11.35	16.90	2.96	18
Punjab	11	6.23	29.16	22.93	15.91	8.36	53
Rajasthan	26	3.95	19.37	15.42	8.30	2.08	25
Tamil Nadu	13	13.60	50.31	36.71	21.36	5.96	28
Uttar Pradesh	54	4.39	24.40	20.01	9.43	3.60	38
West Bengal	16	10.08	35.47	25.39	16.38	6.17	38

Source: *Census of India*, 1971, Special Tables for Scheduled Castes.

Table 5.2

State-wise Educational Growth of the Scheduled Castes (1981)

State	Number of Districts	Percentage of Literacy among SCs in Districts						
		Lowest	Highest	Range	Median	Median Deviation	CRV	% of Growth in Literacy (1971–81)
	(1)	(2)	(3)	(4)	(5)	(6)	(7)	(8)
Andhra Pradesh	22	7.35	28.77	21.42	11.08	6.21	56	65.48
Bihar	31	5.95	24.37	18.42	10.22	3.05	30	59.26
Gujarat	18	21.89	62.54	40.65	37.38	11.40	30	43.44
Haryana	12	10.91	28.83	17.92	21.07	5.70	27	59.92
Karnataka	19	10.41	32.82	22.41	19.50	4.58	23	48.23
Kerala	11	41.93	71.77	29.84	58.15	7.37	13	39.17
Madhya Pradesh	45	4.66	39.80	35.14	17.66	6.39	38	51.88
Maharashtra	25	18.94	46.42	27.48	35.41	6.61	19	40.68
Orissa	13	15.59	28.80	13.21	22.71	3.77	17	43.56
Punjab	12	9.24	35.70	26.46	24.37	9.72	40	47.85
Rajasthan	26	6.74	24.24	17.50	13.49	3.44	26	53.72
Tamil Nadu	15	17.10	57.73	40.63	28.33	6.72	24	35.98
Uttar Pradesh	56	6.93	32.30	20.07	14.94	5.28	35	46.67
West Bengal	15	14.79	33.29	18.50	22.48	5.02	22	36.91

Source: *Census of India*, 1981, Primary Census Abstract, Scheduled Castes.

We have seen in Chapter 4 that the educational growth of the Scheduled Castes in the various states is correlated with the educational growth of the rest of the population in the respective states. Such a relationship is generally true of any state when the districts are treated as units, although the coefficients of correlation in each state are smaller than in the country as a whole. However, except in Madhya Pradesh, Rajasthan and West Bengal in 1971, and Madhya Pradesh, Rajasthan and Tamil Nadu in 1981 where the coefficients range from small to medium degrees, in the rest of the states they range from high to very high degrees (Table 5.3). Thus, by and large, in any state the Scheduled Castes residing in districts which are generally more advanced in literacy have a better chance of a more rapid growth in literacy. This trend explains

Table 5.3

Coefficients of Correlation of the Percentage of Literate Scheduled Castes with the Variables of the Percentage of Literate Non-Scheduled Castes, and the Population of Scheduled Castes and Scheduled Tribes in 1971 and 1981

| State | Percentage of Literate SCs Correlated with | | | | | |
| | Percentage of Literate Non-SCs | | Percentage of SC Population | | Percentage of ST Population | |
	1971 (1)	1981 (2)	1971 (3)	1981 (4)	1971 (5)	1981 (6)
Andhra Pradesh	0.898	0.780	−0.464	−0.361	0.329	−0.308
Bihar	0.706	0.609	−0.395	−0.309	−0.493	0.366
Gujarat	0.690	0.659	−0.430	−0.457	0.389	0.476
Haryana	0.607	0.615	−0.571	−0.650	NA	NA
Karnataka	0.742	0.733	−0.435	−0.600	NA	NA
Kerala	0.867	0.900	0.067	−0.391	NA	NA
Madhya Pradesh	0.571	0.588	−0.315	−0.280	0.004	0.121
Maharashtra	0.704	0.698	−0.665	−0.369	0.064	0.285
Orissa	0.703	0.621	−0.060	−0.203	0.319	−0.203
Punjab	0.745	0.895	0.191	0.175	NA	NA
Rajasthan	0.377	0.547	−0.138	−0.190	0.133	−0.268
Tamil Nadu	0.714	0.596	0.066	0.246	NA	NA
Uttar Pradesh	0.865	0.884	−0.144	−0.252	NA	NA
West Bengal	0.465	0.246	−0.374	−0.271	−0.341	−0.229
India (States as units)	0.925	0.925	−0.365	−0.292	−0.048	−0.090

Source: *Census of India*, Union Primary Census Abstract, and Special Tables for Scheduled Castes and for Scheduled Tribes, 1971; and Primary Census Abstract, for General Population, for Scheduled Castes, and for Scheduled Tribes, 1981.

why the inequalities in literacy of the Scheduled Castes between the most advanced and least advanced districts are widening.

Among the states where these coefficients of correlation are relatively weak (as in Madhya Pradesh and Rajasthan), they have increased in strength; in Tamil Nadu and West Bengal, they have decreased in strength from 1971 to 1981. It may be pointed out in this context that Tamil Nadu and West Bengal are among the former economically more advanced states which have experienced a deceleration in their economic growth during the 1970s (Dandekar, 1988, p. 50).

The constraint exerted by the percentage of the Scheduled Caste population on their progress in literacy, which is found to be of a small degree in the country as a whole, is also found to some extent in the various states (Table 5.3). But in some of the states (such as, Haryana and Maharashtra in 1971 and Haryana and Karnataka in 1981), the negative correlations between the percentage of literacy among the Scheduled Castes and the percentage of their population in the total are appreciably higher.

In the states where there is a substantial percentage of Scheduled Tribes, there is also some noticeable degree of correlation between the percentage of the literacy of the Scheduled Castes and the percentage of population of the Scheduled Tribes. However, the coefficients of correlation in most cases are small or negligible and they are in different directions. Such a pattern agrees with our finding that in the country as a whole there is hardly any correlation between the percentage of literacy among the Scheduled Castes and the population percentage of the Scheduled Tribes.

Educational Development

As in the case of the states, similarly, in the districts of a state, the scores on the index of educational equality of the Scheduled Castes (representing their development) vary widely both in 1971 and 1981 (Tables 5.4 and 5.5). The range of variation in a state in most cases has widened from 1971 to 1981. The relative positions of the states in 1971 and 1981 in terms of their IEE scores have remained more or less the same so that the districts at the top of the range continue to progress rapidly, while those at the bottom are relatively slower. It may be noted that in some districts of Gujarat, Madhya Pradesh and Maharashtra, the Scheduled Castes

Table 5.4

State-wise Educational Development of the Scheduled Castes (1971)

State	IEE Scores of SCs in Districts					
	Lowest	Highest	Rånge	Median	Median Deviation	CRV
	(1)	(2)	(3)	(4)	(5)	(6)
Andhra Pradesh	17	61	44	37	10.86	29
Bihar	20	64	44	29	7.59	26
Gujarat	38	134	96	76	22.48	30
Haryana	34	58	24	48	7.66	16
Karnataka	27	58	31	38	6.46	17
Kerala	40	75	35	65	9.10	14
Madhya Pradesh	17	165	148	48	21.63	45
Maharashtra	43	115	82	70	12.29	18
Orissa	47	95	48	58	13.12	23
Punjab	21	64	43	38	11.05	29
Rajasthan	25	76	51	45	9.58	21
Tamil Nadu	33	86	53	53	8.90	17
Uttar Pradesh	25	64	39	42	7.72	18
West Bengal	27	90	63	58	14.50	25

Source: *Census of India*, 1971, Union Primary Census Abstract, and Special Tables for Scheduled Castes.

have even stolen a march over the rest of the population in their progress in literacy (as indicated by IEE scores above 100).

However, in spite of the fact that the range of IEE scores in the districts has widened in most states, the coefficients of relative variation have narrowed from 1971 to 1981. Thus the pattern of variation of IEE scores is analogous with that of the percentage of literacy.

There is, naturally, a high degree of correlation between the percentage of literacy of the Scheduled Castes (educational growth) and their IEE scores (educational development) as can be seen from Table 5.6. In most districts the coefficients of correlation are of very high degrees. But, in some states, they border on the moderate, while in Orissa they are practically non-existent both in 1971 and 1981 (we shall return to the case of Orissa shortly). However, this pattern confirms the high degree of correlation found in the country as a whole when the states are treated as units.

The percentage of literacy among the non-Scheduled Castes has

Table 5.5
State-wise Educational Development of the Scheduled Castes (1981)

State	IEE Scores of SCs in Districts					
	Lowest	Highest	Range	Median	Median Deviation	CRV
	(1)	(2)	(3)	(4)	(5)	(6)
Andhra Pradesh	34	88	54	50	11.51	23
Bihar	23	69	46	34	8.30	24
Gujarat	59	135	76	96	19.68	20
Haryana	30	78	48	52	10.05	19
Karnataka	36	69	33	44	8.40	19
Kerala	68	88	20	77	5.76	7
Madhya Pradesh	29	164	135	61	21.63	35
Maharashtra	61	174	113	79	13.37	17
Orissa	51	97	46	67	11.38	17
Punjab	27	77	50	49	14.54	30
Rajasthan	28	82	54	58	9.85	17
Tamil Nadu	39	90	51	61	10.35	17
Uttar Pradesh	25	80	55	52	9.05	17
West Bengal	31	86	55	65	13.18	20

Source: *Census of India*, 1981, Primary Census Abstract, General Population, and Scheduled Castes.

been regarded in our study as an index of the educational advancement of a state or district as a whole and, hence, as an indicator of the effect of planning. Therefore, the correlation between the IEE scores and the percentage of literacy among the non-Scheduled Castes in a district gives us an idea about the impact of educational planning on the educational development (IEE scores) of the Scheduled Castes. In the country as a whole, as already pointed out, there is a moderate degree of correlation (0.475 and 0.455 in 1971 and 1981 respectively) between these variables, which shows a declining trend.

However, when we look at the states as universes and the districts as units, the correlations between the IEE scores and the percentage of literacy among the non-Scheduled Castes shows a highly variable pattern. Both in 1971 and in 1981 the coefficients of correlations vary from highly positive to highly negative degrees, and in most states there is a similarity between the coefficients in 1971 and 1981 (Table 5.6).

The coefficients are highly positive in Andhra Pradesh and

Table 5.6

Correlation Coefficients of the IEE Scores with the Percentage of Literate Scheduled Castes, Literate Non-Scheduled Castes and Population of Scheduled Castes and Scheduled Tribes in 1971 and 1981

State	IEE Scores Correlated with							
	Percentage of Literate SCs		Percentage of Literate Non-SCs		Percentage of SC Population		Percentage of ST Population	
	1971 (1)	1981 (2)	1971 (3)	1981 (4)	1971 (5)	1981 (6)	1971 (7)	1981 (8)
Andhra Pradesh	0.881	0.820	0.601	0.317	−0.636	−0.581	0.569	0.014
Bihar	0.814	0.771	0.203	0.013	−0.694	−0.706	0.650	0.626
Gujarat	0.847	0.820	0.348	0.230	−0.509	−0.591	0.587	0.723
Haryana	0.714	0.895	0.000	0.448	−0.571	−0.874	NA	NA
Karnataka	0.582	0.695	−0.025	0.091	−0.175	−0.386	NA	NA
Kerala	0.915	0.855	0.697	0.609	−0.019	−0.582	NA	NA
Madhya Pradesh	0.825	0.647	0.099	−0.158	−0.586	−0.655	0.373	0.476
Maharashtra	0.796	0.757	0.275	0.215	−0.695	−0.408	0.360	0.665
Orissa	−0.088	−0.027	−0.714	−0.731	−0.473	−0.346	0.929	0.841
Punjab	0.945	0.958	0.555	0.769	0.118	0.049	NA	NA
Rajasthan	0.627	0.711	−0.389	−0.078	−0.495	−0.475	0.429	0.452
Tamil Nadu	0.703	0.636	0.176	0.011	−0.170	−0.082	NA	NA
Uttar Pradesh	0.812	0.752	0.461	0.447	−0.242	−0.508	NA	NA
West Bengal	0.624	0.529	−0.318	−0.607	0.015	−0.014	0.021	0.082
India (states as units)	0.741	0.718	0.475	0.455	−0.486	−0.640	0.459	0.501

Source: *Census of India*, Union Primary Census Abstract, and Special Tables for Scheduled Castes, and for Scheduled Tribes, 1971; and Primary Census Abstract, for General Population, for Scheduled Castes, and for Scheduled Tribes, 1981.

Kerala in 1971 and in Kerala and Punjab in 1981, and they are moderately positive in Punjab and Uttar Pradesh in 1971 and in Haryana and Uttar Pradesh in 1981. On the other hand, they are highly negative in Orissa both in 1971 and 1981 and in West Bengal in 1981. In the rest of the states, the coefficients are low or negligible whether they are positive or negative.

Two general observations can be made about the overall pattern of correlation between the percentage of literacy among the non-Scheduled Castes and the IEE scores of the Scheduled Castes in the various states. First, whereas there is a high degree of correlation between the educational growth of the non-Scheduled Castes and that of the Scheduled Castes, there is hardly any or a small degree of correlation between the former variable and the educational development of Scheduled Castes. Second, in most cases, the strength of the correlation has declined from 1971 to 1981. The broad pattern supports the respective findings for the country as a whole in 1971 and 1981.

When we compare the two sets of correlations in the states—those between the IEE scores and literacy among the non-Scheduled Castes, on the one hand, and between the IEE scores and literacy among the Scheduled Castes on the other (i.e., Table 6.6, columns 3 and 1 for 1971 and columns 4 and 2 for 1981), it is found that they are highly correlated ($r = 0.820$ and 0.858 in 1971 and 1981 respectively). These trends would indicate that when the educational growth of a state is highly associated with the educational development of the Scheduled Castes (as in Punjab), the correlation between the educational growth of the Scheduled Castes and their educational development is also very high. On the other hand, when the educational growth of a state detracts from the educational development of the Scheduled Castes (as in Orissa), the correlation between the educational growth of the Scheduled Castes and their educational development is also low; in the instant case, it is nil. Therefore, it seems that, in some of the states, the educational advancement of the rest of the population rather than inducing a trickle-down effect upon the educational development of the Scheduled Castes, actually pushes them back. Even so, because of their highly favourable structural situation, (presence of the highest percentage of Scheduled Tribes in the state) the Scheduled Castes in Orissa have fared relatively better as compared with Scheduled Castes, in the other states.

Nevertheless, it needs to be pointed out that despite the positive correlation between the sets of correlations in the states—i.e., between (a) the IEE scores of the Scheduled Castes and literacy among the non-Scheduled Castes, on the one hand, and (b) the IEE scores of the Scheduled Castes and literacy among them, on the other—the strengths of the former set of correlations are far lower than those of the latter set (in Table 5.6, compare columns 1 and 2 with columns 3 and 4 respectively). This difference, to some extent, can be accounted for by the structural factors discussed in the previous chapter, which are represented by the population percentages of the Scheduled Castes and Tribes residing in the state.

When we consider the relationship of the IEE scores with the population percentage of the Scheduled Castes in the states (Table 5.6, columns 5 and 6 for 1971 and 1981 respectively), we find that there is, with a few exceptions, a moderate to high degree of negative correlation in most cases. In at least half the number of states, the values of the coefficients have increased markedly from 1971 to 1981; where they have declined, the decline is small or insignificant. These trends agree with the all-India findings, the corresponding coefficients of correlations already noticed being -0.486 and -0.640 in 1971 and 1981 respectively. Thus, in the states also, the educational development of the Scheduled Castes is hampered by the higher percentages of their population.

There are, however, important exceptions to this observation, such as the states of Punjab, Tamil Nadu and West Bengal. But these states do not share any bond which can be attributed to their common situation in this particular case. Punjab is economically the most advanced state and Tamil Nadu and West Bengal are the two states among the former relatively advanced states which are experiencing a decline in their economic situations. We also notice that in the case of Punjab, the practically non-existing correlation between the IEE scores and the population of the Scheduled Castes (Table 5.6, columns 5 and 6) is accompanied by high to very high degrees of coefficients of correlation between the IEE scores and literacy among the Scheduled Castes (columns 1 and 2) and between the former and literacy among the non-Scheduled Castes (columns 3 and 4). On the other hand, in the case of Tamil Nadu and West Bengal, the negligible coefficients of correlations in columns 5 and 6 (Table 5.6) are accompanied by much lower coefficients in columns 1 and 2 as well as 3 and 4.

There are also moderate to high degrees of correlation between the IEE scores of the Scheduled Castes and the percentages of the population of Scheduled Tribes in most of the states in which the Scheduled Tribes are found in appreciable proportions (Table 5.6, columns 7 and 8). The coefficients in this case are positive, indicating that the Scheduled Castes show better educational development if they are surrounded by Scheduled Tribes. This positive influence of the proportion of Scheduled Tribe population has increased from 1971 to 1981 in most of the states, which agrees with the all-India situation. Again, West Bengal is a notable exception in both these respects. Orissa is also worth noting, but for different reasons. This state shows extremely high degrees of correlation between the IEE scores of the Scheduled Castes and the percentage of population of the Scheduled Tribes both in 1971 and 1981 (although with a declining trend). Orissa also differs from all the other states as it has no correlation between the IEE scores of the Scheduled Castes and their percentage of literacy (columns 1 and 2) and the relatively highest negative correlation between the IEE scores of the Scheduled Castes and the percentage of literacy of non-Scheduled Castes (columns 3 and 4).

Table 5.6 shows that some of the states tend to depart rather markedly from the general pattern in almost all the columns. They include Karnataka, Orissa, Tamil Nadu and West Bengal. Some of the states also show marked differences only in one set of correlations, such as Madhya Pradesh which shows hardly any correlation between the IEE scores of the Scheduled Castes and literacy among the non-Scheduled Castes (columns 3 and 4), and Punjab which does not show any correlation between the IEE scores of the Scheduled Castes and their percentage of population (columns 5 and 6). It would be interesting to follow up these exceptions as we consider the other developmental variables.

In summary, it may be stated that the same patterns of educational growth and development of the Scheduled Castes noticed in the country as a whole when the states are treated as units are also seen in the several states when the districts are treated as units. There is a wide variation in both the growth and development of the Scheduled Castes in education from district to district and the distance between the extremities has increased. There is also a high degree of correlation between the educational growth of the Scheduled Castes and that of the non-Scheduled Castes. But the correlation between the educational development of Scheduled

Castes and that of the non-Scheduled Castes shows a highly variable pattern in different states, the coefficients ranging from highly positive to highly negative degrees. In this respect, although the states for the most part do not exactly replicate the all-India pattern, the total pattern is in agreement with the moderate level of correlation found in the latter. The moderate to high degree of negative correlation which is found between the educational development of the Scheduled Castes and the percentage of their population, and the moderate to high degree of positive correlation found between the educational development of the Scheduled Castes and the population of the Scheduled Tribes which are noticeable in most of the states, are in accord with the all-India findings.

Urban Growth and Development

Urban Growth

In evaluating the data presented here, it must be borne in mind that the totally rural or urban districts which are found in some of the states have been omitted. Despite this, there is a great deal of state-wise variation, as in the case of the literacy and urbanization of the Scheduled Castes. We should first consider the percentage of urban population among the Scheduled Castes in the various states. In most of the states there is a wide range of variation in the percentage of urban population among the Scheduled Castes in the districts (Table 5.7). The range of variation in 1971 is especially small in Haryana, Punjab and West Bengal, and rather small in Kerala and Orissa, whereas it is extremely large in Gujarat, Madhya Pradesh and Maharashtra.

However, the coefficient of relative variation (CRV) provides a more valid basis of comparison. Accordingly, Haryana and Punjab have the lowest CRV values of 18 per cent each while Bihar and Uttar Pradesh have the two highest values of 117 and 103 per cent respectively (Table 5.7, column 6). In comparison with the variation in their literacy (Table 5.1), the variation in the urbanization of the Scheduled Castes in the districts of any state is much wider. Even though the median values on urbanization are smaller as compared with those on education, the ranges of variation as well as the

Table 5.7
State-wise Urbanization of the Scheduled Castes (1971)

State	Percentage of Urban Population among SCs in Districts					
	Lowest	Highest	Range	Median	Median Deviation	CRV
	(1)	(2)	(3)	(4)	(5)	(6)
Andhra Pradesh	2.99	47.85	44.86	8.87	5.66	64
Bihar	2.16	36.88	32.72	5.04	5.90	117
Gujarat	4.99	66.57	61.58	18.94	8.92	47
Haryana	9.08	14.69	5.61	10.11	1.82	18
Karnataka	6.27	38.11	31.84	13.77	4.61	33
Kerala	3.90	23.69	19.79	7.24	4.80	66
Madhya Pradesh	0.51	51.53	51.02	9.43	6.02	64
Maharashtra	6.76	54.86	48.10	17.27	9.52	55
Orissa	2.27	22.61	20.34	5.23	3.27	63
Punjab	6.82	20.59	13.77	14.43	2.55	18
Rajasthan	4.05	38.90	34.85	12.00	5.13	43
Tamil Nadu	4.87	50.75	45.88	14.10	7.31	52
Uttar Pradesh	0.59	38.83	38.25	4.82	4.98	103
West Bengal	1.29	15.05	13.76	8.30	3.46	42

Source: *Census of India*, 1971, Primary Census Abstract, and Special Tables for Scheduled Castes.

CRV values in respect of the former variable are higher in every state. Therefore, the urbanization of the Scheduled Castes in the different districts of a state is far more uneven than their literacy rates.

The urban population among the Scheduled Castes in the country as a whole has grown by 34 per cent from 1971 to 1981 and, as one might expect, the growth rates of the percentage of urban population vary considerably from state to state, from 16.67 per cent in Tamil Nadu to 51.34 per cent in West Bengal (Table 5.8). By and large, this variation is related to the variation in the urban growth rates of the non-Scheduled Caste population, although the overall growth rate of this category (18 per cent) is much lower than that of the Scheduled Castes (34 per cent). However, the case of West Bengal is a notable exception; whereas the percentage of the urban population of the non-Scheduled Castes has grown the least in this state (4 per cent) from 1971 to 1981, that of the Scheduled Castes has grown the most (51 per cent). One of the major reasons for this peculiar situation is that, to

Table 5.8

State-wise Urbanization of the Scheduled Castes (1981)

State	Percentage of Urban Population among SCs in Districts					
	Lowest	Highest	Range	Median	Median Deviation	CRV	% of Growth in Urban Population of SCs (1971–81)
	(1)	(2)	(3)	(4)	(5)	(6)	(7)
Andhra Pradesh	5.56	38.19	32.63	12.53	4.65	37	30.14
Bihar	2.18	45.19	43.01	6.29	5.39	86	31.27
Gujarat	7.85	72.31	64.46	24.24	10.92	46	20.05
Haryana	8.63	31.16	22.53	15.07	4.08	27	44.95
Karnataka	8.07	51.13	43.06	16.53	6.14	37	30.54
Kerala	1.80	27.20	25.40	8.83	6.04	68	25.02
Madhya Pradesh	1.12	58.80	57.68	12.44	7.54	61	38.69
Maharashtra	8.22	64.79	56.57	21.57	10.23	47	21.77
Orissa	4.28	32.01	27.73	9.23	4.05	44	49.92
Punjab	10.37	25.69	15.32	17.46	3.24	19	27.34
Rajasthan	7.61	45.10	37.49	15.23	5.74	38	25.70
Tamil Nadu	5.71	51.17	45.46	14.64	8.33	57	16.67
Uttar Pradesh	1.48	46.11	44.63	8.27	6.77	82	38.36
West Bengal	1.75	23.85	22.10	9.42	5.03	53	51.34

Source: *Census of India*, Primary Census Abstract, Scheduled Castes, 1981; Special Tables for Scheduled Castes, 1971.

begin with, in 1971 there was too great a disparity between the urbanization of the Scheduled Castes and that of the rest of the population and the base figure in 1971 was rather small.

With the relatively more rapid growth of urbanization of the Scheduled Castes from 1971 to 1981, the inequalities in the percentages of the urban population of the Scheduled Castes between the most urbanized and the least urbanized districts in respect of the percentage of urban population of the Scheduled Castes have further widened in most of the states (compare column 3 of Tables 5.7 and 5.8). Andhra Pradesh, however, is a notable exception. The CRV values in many of the states have come down in 1981, especially where they were very high in 1971; but where they were low in 1971, they have increased in some cases.

In the case of education, we have seen that the growth of the Scheduled Castes is associated with that of the rest of the population. In the case of urbanization, too, a similar trend is visible although the strengths of the coefficients of correlations in most cases are somewhat lower (compare Tables 5.9 and 5.3), which agrees with the all-India findings. Thus, in every state, we find that the growth in urbanization of the Scheduled Castes is correlated with the growth of urbanization of the rest of the population (Table 5.9). It is also interesting to see from the table that in most of the states (and especially in those where the coefficients were smaller to begin with), the strength of this relationship has increased from 1971 to 1981. The trickle-down effect of overall growth can be seen in the urbanization of the Scheduled Castes also. The coefficients of correlation, however, are relatively much lower in some states. This is especially true in Punjab where it is considerably much lower than it is for the country as a whole, both in 1971 and 1981.

The relative size of the Scheduled Caste population (Table 5.9, columns 3 and 4) has checked their urbanization in varying degrees in most of the states, except Punjab and Rajasthan both in 1971 and 1981, and Haryana in 1971. The constraint of numbers is especially high in Orissa, both in 1971 and 1981 and in West Bengal in 1971. The relative size of the population of the Scheduled Tribes (Table 5.9, columns 5 and 6) has also been a factor in the urbanization of the Scheduled Castes except in Bihar where it has played a moderately positive role; in other states, it has played a minor role whether positive or negative.

On the whole, therefore, despite some influence of the structural factors, the urbanization of the Scheduled Castes is highly correlated with the general urbanization of the state.

Table 5.9

Coefficients of Correlation of the Percentage of Urban Scheduled Caste Population with the Variables of the Percentage of Urban Population of the Non-Scheduled Castes and the Population of Scheduled Castes and Scheduled Tribes in 1971 and 1981

State	Variables Correlated with Percentage of Urban SCs					
	Percentage of Urban Non-SCs		Percentage of SC Population		Percentage of ST Population	
	1971 (1)	1981 (2)	1971 (3)	1981 (4)	1971 (5)	1981 (6)
Andhra Pradesh	0.749	0.765	−0.513	−0.352	0.400	0.070
Bihar	0.865	0.887	−0.453	−0.259	0.517	0.507
Gujarat	0.862	0.804	−0.230	−0.212	0.003	0.007
Haryana	0.714	0.741	0.250	−0.371	NA	NA
Karnataka	0.723	0.772	−0.314	−0.368	NA	NA
Kerala	0.964	0.927	−0.261	−0.464	NA	NA
Madhya Pradesh	0.769	0.735	−0.025	−0.203	−0.251	−0.072
Maharashtra	0.679	0.782	−0.535	−0.363	0.160	0.409
Orissa	0.841	0.709	−0.610	−0.791	0.209	0.352
Punjab	0.655	0.692	0.291	0.224	NA	NA
Rajasthan	0.878	0.897	0.115	0.154	−0.336	−0.283
Tamil Nadu	0.841	0.871	−0.044	0.046	NA	NA
Uttar Pradesh	0.874	0.860	−0.242	−0.237	NA	NA
West Bengal	0.629	0.793	−0.606	−0.496	−0.282	−0.239
India (states as units)	0.778	0.842	−0.360	−0.187	0.719	0.659

Source: *Census of India*, Union Primary Census Abstract, and Special Tables for Scheduled Castes, and for Scheduled Tribes, 1971; and Primary Census Abstract, for General Population, for Scheduled Castes, and for Scheduled Tribes, 1981.

Urban Development

As in the case of urbanization or urban growth, there is also a wide variation in the urban development (IEU scores) of the Scheduled Castes in the various districts of a state both in 1971 (Table 5.10) and in 1981 (Table 5.11). Some of the ranges of variation (column 3), especially those in Gujarat, Madhya Pradesh, Maharashtra, Orissa and Rajasthan, are very large.

An index score of more than 100 in a district would mean that the Scheduled Castes in that district are over-represented in the

Table 5.10
State-wise Urban Development of the Scheduled Castes (1971)

State	IEU Scores of SCs in Districts					
	Lowest	Highest	Range	Median	Median Deviation	CRV
	(1)	(2)	(3)	(4)	(5)	(6)
Andhra Pradesh	19	107	88	53	16.63	31
Bihar	38	133	95	65	18.97	29
Gujarat	55	130	75	86	19.20	22
Haryana	40	87	39	59	10.84	18
Karnataka	48	93	45	63	12.37	20
Kerala	48	88	40	56	7.58	14
Madhya Pradesh	33	223	190	71	26.19	37
Maharashtra	50	171	121	101	27.06	27
Orissa	37	155	118	86	21.42	25
Punjab	38	73	35	61	9.33	15
Rajasthan	47	156	109	78	18.71	24
Tamil Nadu	27	104	77	53	15.06	28
Uttar Pradesh	16	93	77	47	16.84	36
West Bengal	34	120	86	37	22.87	62

Source: *Census of India*, 1971, Union Primary Census Abstract, and Special Tables for Scheduled Castes.

urban areas. In most of the states there are at least a few such districts (see column 2 of Tables 5.10 and 5.11 which gives the highest IEU score in a district). The number of states with districts with an over-representation of Scheduled Castes in urban areas has increased from 9 in 1971 to 11 in 1981.

Although a few of the excessively large ranges of variation in the IEU scores have narrowed down from 1971 to 1981, the tendency has been for the ranges to widen over the decade. The same districts occupying the top few rungs in 1971 have continued to do so in 1981 and, similarly, the districts in the lower ranges in 1971 have maintained their relative positions in 1981 also (not shown in the tables). Therefore, inequalities between the most developed and the least developed districts in terms of urban representation of the Scheduled Castes have widened.

In overall patterns of inequalities in the IEU scores, as indicated by the CRV values (Tables 5.10 and 5.11, column 6), the states show a wide variation. In 1971, the CRV value of West Bengal seems to have been too aberrant and, accordingly, it has shown the

Table 5.11
State-wise Urban Development of the Scheduled Castes (1981)

State	IEU Scores of SCs in Districts					
	Lowest	Highest	Range	Median	Median Deviation	CRV
	(1)	(2)	(3)	(4)	(5)	(6)
Andhra Pradesh	39	124	85	59	15.64	27
Bihar	38	116	78	67	16.08	25
Gujarat	58	183	125	99	22.47	23
Haryana	42	111	69	69	13.30	20
Karnataka	51	120	69	72	12.77	18
Kerala	36	87	51	64	10.00	16
Madhya Pradesh	40	154	114	78	25.31	25
Maharashtra	52	221	169	101	25.66	25
Orissa	47	159	112	91	22.17	24
Punjab	42	82	40	63	7.11	11
Rajasthan	55	188	133	85	17.94	21
Tamil Nadu	28	106	78	51	13.66	27
Uttar Pradesh	19	99	80	53	17.51	33
West Bengal	15	106	91	50	17.65	35

Source: *Census of India*, 1981, Primary Census Abstract, for General Population, and for Scheduled Castes.

highest decline from 1971 to 1981. On the whole, also, there has been a general decline in CRV values from 1971 to 1981. In terms of CRV values, four states (Kerala, Punjab, Haryana and Karnataka) have maintained the lowest four positions both in 1971 and 1981. It would appear that in these states there is a relatively greater degree of inter-district equity in their urban representation for the Scheduled Castes. On the other hand, West Bengal, Uttar Pradesh and Andhra Pradesh, both in 1971 and 1981, Madhya Pradesh in 1971 and Tamil Nadu in 1981, with higher CRV values, would appear to be relatively more inequitable in this respect.

Let us now look at the correlation between the IEU scores of the Scheduled Castes (or their urban development) and some of the significant variables shown in Table 5.12. We have already seen in the foregoing that the IEE scores in most states, show high to very high degrees of correlation with the percentage of literacy of the Scheduled Castes. Analogously, when we correlate the IEU scores of the Scheduled Castes with the percentage of their urban population, the coefficients become far lower (columns 1 and 2). They

Table 5.12

Correlation Coefficients of the IEU Scores of the Scheduled Castes with the Percentage of the Urban Scheduled Castes, the Urban Non-Scheduled Castes and the Scheduled Caste and Scheduled Tribe Population

State	IEU Scores Correlated with							
	Percentage of Urban SCs		Percentage of Urban Non-SCs		Percentage of SC Population		Percentage of ST Population	
	1971 (1)	1981 (2)	1971 (3)	1981 (4)	1971 (5)	1981 (6)	1971 (7)	1981 (8)
Andhra Pradesh	0.699	0.682	0.127	0.128	−0.327	−0.465	0.308	0.402
Bihar	0.613	0.561	0.250	0.162	−0.725	−0.651	0.520	0.386
Gujarat	0.366	0.335	0.009	−0.214	−0.496	−0.453	0.315	0.649
Haryana	−0.036	0.413	−0.536	−0.182	−0.857	−0.587	NA	NA
Karnataka	0.625	0.667	−0.002	0.112	−0.523	−0.575	NA	NA
Kerala	0.176	0.445	−0.248	0.145	−0.248	−0.536	NA	NA
Madhya Pradesh	0.358	0.346	−0.214	−0.306	−0.588	−0.631	0.437	0.423
Maharashtra	0.648	0.484	0.057	−0.105	−0.770	−0.674	0.384	0.468
Orissa	0.220	0.582	−0.297	−0.099	−0.511	−0.676	0.890	0.912
Punjab	0.273	−0.119	−0.445	−0.699	−0.136	−0.014	NA	NA
Rajasthan	−0.024	−0.122	−0.425	−0.450	−0.346	−0.371	0.380	0.512
Tamil Nadu	0.643	0.507	0.209	0.125	−0.390	−0.414	NA	NA
Uttar Pradesh	0.506	0.597	0.063	0.149	−0.374	−0.379	NA	NA
West Bengal	0.447	0.043	−0.238	−0.539	−0.456	−0.479	0.162	0.289
India (states as units)	0.413	0.409	−0.084	−0.031	−0.745	−0.767	0.719	0.659

Source: *Census of India*, Union Primary Census Abstract, and Special Tables for Scheduled Castes, and for Scheduled Tribes, 1971; and Primary Census Abstract, for General Population for Scheduled Castes, and for Scheduled Tribes, 1981.

range from practically negligible in some cases through low, moderate and high in a few cases. The overall pattern agrees with the all-India situation where also these coefficients in 1971 and 1981 were only of the order of 0.413 and 0.409 respectively.

Thus, insofar as the urbanization of the Scheduled Castes is concerned, their development is not quite in keeping with their growth. Their development is even more out of step with the urban growth of the rest of the population (columns 3 and 4). The coefficients of correlations between the IEU scores and the percentage of urban population of the non-Scheduled Castes are, in most cases, negative and negligible or small. In Haryana in 1971, and in West Bengal and Punjab in 1981, they are moderate to highly negative. In these states the growth in urbanization of the state as a whole has been detrimental to the urban development of the Scheduled Castes, while in no state has the general urbanization of the state contributed appreciably to the urban development of the Scheduled Castes.

The population percentage of the Scheduled Castes in the districts has turned out to be a negative correlate of their urban development in all the states. The coefficients of correlation are moderate to high in most states. When they are not very high—say, below -0.700—they have tended to increase from 1971 to 1981, which implies that with the growing urbanization of a district their own population size is becoming a growing hurdle against the urban development of the Scheduled Castes. In this respect also, what is happening in the country as a whole is being replicated in most of the states. The case of Punjab, however, is a notable exception. Even in the case of education, it may be recalled, the population percentage of the Scheduled Castes has not affected their educational development (IEE scores) in this state.

The population percentage of the Scheduled Tribes in a district bears a positive correlation with the IEU scores (Table 5.12, columns 7 and 8). This is so in all the states where there is a substantial Scheduled Tribe population. The correlation is especially high in the case of Orissa. Again, it may be recalled that in Orissa the coefficient of correlation between the IEE scores of the Scheduled Castes and the percentage of Scheduled Tribe population is also extremely high.

To conclude, let us make a few general observations. Both in urban growth and development the different districts of a state are highly uneven and the extremities have widened from 1971 to 1981. The urban growth of the Scheduled Castes in the districts is highly correlated with the urban growth of the rest of the population and somewhat constrained by the higher percentage of their own population. Their urban development is only moderately correlated with their urban growth and even negatively correlated with the urban growth of the rest of the population, although the strengths of these correlations are rather weak in most cases. But it is important to emphasize that the general socio-economic development of the district has not proved advantageous to the urban development of the Scheduled Castes. More than in the case of their educational development, the size of their population has been an important constraint on their urban development. On the other hand, the presence of the Scheduled Tribes has facilitated the urban development of the Scheduled Castes, which is true even in the case of their educational development. In all these respects the states, by and large, replicate the developmental situation experienced by the Scheduled Castes in the country.

Industrial Growth and Development

As pointed out in the previous chapter, industrial growth and development is measured by the proportion of non-agricultural occupations since, in the initial stages of economic development, an economy with preponderantly agricultural occupations transforms itself into one with increasing proportions of non-agricultural occupations (including both secondary and tertiary occupations). The non-agricultural occupations as a whole bear a high degree of correlation with industrial occupations (those in the manufacturing industries). Only the 1981 Census data will be utilized in this part of our analysis as comparable data applicable to all categories were not available for 1971.

I have departed slightly from the procedure adopted so far to compute the index scores on the equality of industrialization (IEI) inasmuch as the percentage of non-agricultural workers among the Scheduled Castes is divided by the percentage of non-agricultural workers among the non-Scheduled Caste minus the Scheduled Tribe category instead of the entire non-Scheduled Caste category. So, also, instead of correlating the industrial growth or the development of the Scheduled Castes with the industrial growth of the non-Scheduled Castes, it is done with that of the non-Scheduled Caste/Scheduled Tribe category. These modifications, however, do not materially alter the trends.

Industrial Growth

As in the case of literacy and urbanization, so also in the case of the percentage of non-agricultural workers (industrialization) among the Scheduled Castes, there is a wide variation in the different districts of a state in 1981 (Table 5.13). The smallest range which is found in Punjab is 25 and the largest is in Tamil Nadu, which is 90. The extremely high range in Tamil Nadu is due to the Nilgiri district with its extensive plantation activity where the occupations have been returned as belonging to the non-agricultural category. If this district is excluded, the range in Tamil Nadu shrinks to 31 and the position of the highest range goes to Maharashtra with a range of 73. Thus, the ranges in the case of industrialization are even wider than those observed in the case of literacy and urbanization. The CRV values (column 6) are also relatively quite high in most of the states (ranging from 23 in Punjab to 78 in Bihar). The Scheduled Castes in most of the states, therefore, have very uneven prospects of industrialization.

In most of the states, the opportunities of the Scheduled Castes in non-agricultural economic activities are linked with the opportunities of the non-Scheduled Caste/Scheduled Tribe category (Table 5.14, column 1). This is, however, not true of Andhra Pradesh and Punjab, but true to a very much small degree in Kerala and Orissa. Thus, in most of the states, the growth of non-agricultural occupations in general have a trickle-down effect on the Scheduled Castes.

In their industrial growth the Scheduled Castes are also hampered by the size of their own population in various degrees in the different states (Table 5.14, column 2). The disadvantage suffered is high to very high in states such as Bihar ($r = -0.729$), Haryana ($r = -0.762$), Orissa ($r = -0.808$) and West Bengal ($r = -0.646$); the size has mattered little or not at all in Gujarat, Kerala and Punjab. On the other hand, in most of the states where the Scheduled Tribes are found in substantial numbers the Scheduled Castes have fared better in industrialization (Table 5.14, column 3) although the advantage is small.

Table 5.13
State-wise Industrial Growth of the Scheduled Castes (1981)

State	Percentage of Non-Agricultural Workers in Districts					
	Lowest (1)	Highest (2)	Range (3)	Median (4)	Median Deviation (5)	CRV (6)
Andhra Pradesh	6.82	43.39	36.57	12.33	4.43	36
Bihar	5.56	75.34	69.78	11.21	8.71	78
Gujarat	3.61	72.83	69.22	36.70	13.75	37
Haryana	22.14	60.88	38.74	36.73	11.40	31
Karnataka	13.84	67.56	53.72	21.24	10.66	50
Kerala	23.67	76.50	52.83	37.94	20.44	54
Madhya Pradesh	12.60	56.26	43.66	20.78	8.79	42
Maharashtra	15.63	88.44	72.81	31.50	13.39	43
Orissa	14.59	49.08	34.49	24.12	7.22	30
Punjab	21.75	46.75	25.00	34.17	7.90	23
Rajasthan	13.84	53.32	39.48	30.93	7.21	24
Tamil Nadu	5.46	95.42	89.96*	19.01	10.88	57‡
Uttar Pradesh	4.20	58.00	53.80	15.04	8.17	54
West Bengal	11.92	48.73	36.81	24.07	8.66	36

Source: *Census of India*, 1981, Primary Census Abstract, Scheduled Castes.

* = 31 and ‡ = 33.

Table 5.14
*Coefficients of Correlation of the Percentage of Non-Agricultural Workers
among the Scheduled Castes with the Percentage of Non-Agricultural Workers
among Non-Scheduled Castes/Tribes and of the Population of Scheduled Castes
and Tribes in the Districts in Each State (1981)*

State	Variables Correlated with Percentage of Non-Agricultural Workers among SCs		
	Percentage of Non-Agricultural Workers among Non-SC/STs	Percentage of Population of	
		SCs	STs
	(1)	(2)	(3)
Andhra Pradesh	0.139	−0.474	0.388
Bihar	0.664	−0.729	0.383
Gujarat	0.874	−0.090	0.201
Haryana	0.664	−0.762	NA
Karnataka	0.740	−0.549	NA
Kerala	0.473	−0.118	NA
Madhya Pradesh	0.717	−0.257	0.275
Maharashtra	0.737	−0.284	0.322
Orissa	0.593	−0.808	0.445
Punjab	0.051	0.119	NA
Rajasthan	0.726	−0.251	0.124
Tamil Nadu	0.775	−0.236	NA
Uttar Pradesh	0.836	−0.294	NA
West Bengal	0.636	−0.646	−0.264
India (states as units)	0.709	−0.253	−0.035

Source: *Census of India*, 1981, Primary Census Abstract, for General Population, for Scheduled Castes, and for Scheduled Tribes.

Industrial Development

It has already been pointed out that the industrial development of the Scheduled Castes, which is denoted by their IEI scores, varies widely from state to state. The same picture is conveyed by the median IEI scores in the districts (Table 5.15, column 4). In Haryana and Maharashtra, as indicated by the median scores, the Scheduled Castes are on par with or better than the non-Scheduled Caste/Scheduled Tribe category, in their industrial development. So also in every state, except Punjab, there are one or more districts in which the Scheduled Castes are over-represented in industrialization.

Table 5.15
State-wise Industrial Development of the Scheduled Castes (1981)

State	IEI Scores of SCs in Districts					
	Lowest	Highest	Range	Median	Median Deviation	CRV
	(1)	(2)	(3)	(4)	(5)	(6)
Andhra Pradesh	13	273	260	35.93	23.10	64
Bihar	30	182	152	59.36	18.93	32
Gujarat	10	130	128	88.83	18.85	21
Haryana	68	153	85	99.86	20.60	21
Karnataka	48	110	62	74.63	14.67	20
Kerala	47	158	111	63.63	15.09	24
Madhya Pradesh	50	243	193	78.50	17.89	23
Maharashtra	45	252	207	115.64	29.15	25
Orissa	56	123	67	79.81	14.53	18
Punjab	32	61	29	45.73	7.85	17
Rajasthan	47	121	74	86.51	15.03	18
Tamil Nadu	14	104	90	44.50	14.69	33
Uttar Pradesh	25	113	88	64.97	17.75	27
West Bengal	34	107	73	57.33	15.83	28

Source: *Census of India*, 1981, Primary Census Abstract, for General Population, and for Scheduled Castes.

However, in most states, the differences in the IEI scores of the Scheduled Castes between the district with the highest score and that with the lowest score are very high (Table 5.15, column 3). However, the CRV values are not unduly high (except in the case of Andhra Pradesh).

The IEI scores of the Scheduled Castes are highly correlated with their industrial growth (percentage of non-agricultural occupations) in most of the states except Andhra Pradesh and Punjab; in Kerala and Orissa, the correlations are much reduced (Table 5.16, column 1). But there is hardly any correspondence between the industrial development of the Scheduled Castes and the industrial growth of the non-Scheduled Caste/Scheduled Tribe category (column 2). The relevant coefficients of correlation, in all the states (except Maharashtra) are either small or negligible, and they are negative in as many states as they are positive. Thus in industrial development also, as in educational and urban development, the gains have not accrued to the Scheduled Castes in proportion to the industrial growth of the district although there

Table 5.16

Coefficients of Correlation of IEI Scores of the Scheduled Castes with the Percentage of Non-Agricultural Workers among the Scheduled Castes and the Non-Scheduled Castes/Tribes and with those of the Scheduled Caste and Tribe Population in the Districts in Each State (1981)

State	IEI Scores of SCs Correlated with			
	Percentage of Non-Agricultural Workers among		Percentage of Population of	
	SCs (1)	Non-SC/STs (2)	SCs (3)	STs (4)
Andhra Pradesh	0.139	−0.320	−0.355	0.282
Bihar	0.664	0.029	−0.430	0.494
Gujarat	0.874	0.007	−0.259	0.304
Haryana	0.664	−0.230	−0.685	NA
Karnataka	0.740	0.249	−0.391	NA
Kerala	0.473	0.200	−0.273	NA
Madhya Pradesh	0.717	−0.210	−0.164	0.176
Maharashtra	0.737	0.467	0.066	0.076
Orissa	0.593	−0.390	−0.401	0.335
Punjab	0.082	−0.255	0.140	NA
Rajasthan	0.726	−0.249	−0.150	0.000
Tamil Nadu	0.775	0.114	−0.404	NA
Uttar Pradesh	0.836	0.293	−0.305	NA
West Bengal	0.636	−0.304	−0.704	−0.007
India (states as units)	0.709	0.037	−0.383	0.568

Source: *Census of India*, 1981, Primary Census Abstract, for General Population, for Scheduled Castes, and for Scheduled Tribes.

was a spurt in the industrial development of the Scheduled Castes from 1971–81.

The IEI scores of the Scheduled Castes show different degrees of correlations (mostly negative) with the percentage of their population in different states. Only in Haryana and in West Bengal are the negative coefficients of correlations high. It would, therefore, appear that the size of their population is not as great a hurdle in their industrial development as in their industrial growth. It is also less of a hurdle in industrial development as it is in their educational and urban development. Since our indices are of a coarse nature, it is possible that the percentage of non-agricultural occupations is a much weaker index of advancement than the percentages of literacy and urbanization. That is why the Scheduled Castes are facing a relatively lesser degree of competition from the non-Scheduled Castes/Scheduled Tribes in their industrial development.

The size of the population of the Scheduled Tribes is slightly beneficial to the industrial development of the Scheduled Castes in the various states (Table 5.16, column 4). The trend is the same as the all-India setting with the states as the units but the degree of correlation is much higher at the all-India level.

To sum up, even as regards industrial growth and development, the patterns noticeable in the various states are broadly in agreement with the all-India pattern. Both at the national level and the state levels, the patterns are slightly at variance with the patterns of educational and urban growth and development at the corresponding levels; however, the basic trends are the same.

Synoptic View

Finally, it may be useful to have a synoptic view of the growth and developmental variables, taking education, urbanization and industrialization together. Table 5.17 refers to the growth patterns. It gives the coefficients of correlation of each of the growth variables of the Scheduled Castes with those of their non-Scheduled Caste counterparts and the percentage of the population of the Scheduled Castes in the various states. The coefficients of correlation between the growth variables of the Scheduled Castes and the percentage of the population, although significant for our study, are not shown in the table because of the convenience of presentation and because the Scheduled Tribe population in some of the states is either absent or found in negligible proportions. The different degrees of correlations are given scores as follows:

Degree of Correlation	Score	Description
0 – 1.99	0	Negligible
2 – 3.99	1	Low
4 – 5.99	2	Moderate
6 – 7.99	3	High
8 +	4	Very high

Table 5.17

Scores on the Coefficients of Correlation of Each of the Growth Variables of Education, Urbanization and Industrialization of the Scheduled Castes with the Corresponding Variables of the Non-Scheduled Castes and with the Population Percentage of the Scheduled Castes in the Various States

| State | I. % of Literate SCs Correlated with | | | | II. % of Urban SCs Correlated with | | | | III. % of SC NAWs Correlated with | |
| | % of Literate Non-SCs | | % of SC Population | | Urban Non-SCs | | % of SC Population | | % of Non-SC/ST NAWs | % of SC Population |
	1971 (1)	1981 (2)	1971 (3)	1981 (4)	1971 (5)	1981 (6)	1971 (7)	1981 (8)	1981 (9)	1981 (10)
Andhra Pradesh	4	3	−2	−1	3	3	−2	−1	1	−2
Bihar	3	3	−1	−1	4	4	−2	−1	3	−3
Gujarat	3	3	−2	−2	4	4	−1	−1	4	−0
Haryana	3	3	−2	−3	3	3	1	−1	3	−3
Karnataka	3	3	−2	−3	3	3	−1	−1	3	−2
Kerala	4	4	0	−1	4	4	−1	−2	2	−0
Madhya Pradesh	2	2	−1	−1	3	3	−0	−1	3	−1
Maharashtra	3	3	−3	−1	3	3	−2	−1	3	−1
Orissa	3	3	−0	−1	4	3	−3	−3	2	−4
Punjab	3	4	0	0	3	3	1	1	0	0
Rajasthan	1	2	−0	−0	4	4	0	0	3	−1
Tamil Nadu	3	2	0	1	4	4	0	0	3	−1
Uttar Pradesh	4	4	−0	−1	4	4	−1	−1	4	−1
West Bengal	2	1	−1	−1	3	3	−3	−2	3	−3
India (states as units)	4	4	−1	−1	3	4	−1	−0	3	−1

Source: Table 5.3 for Cols. 1, 2, 3 and 4; Table 5.9 for Cols. 5, 6, 7 and 8; and Table 5.14 for Cols. 9 and 10.

Note: Since the score 0 + or − quantity from 0 to 1.99 degrees, some of the 0 scores in the Table have assumed negative signs.

On the whole, it is obvious that the pattern of correlations in the states with respect to all the three growth variables (sets I, II and III in Table 5.17) are similar. In each column, the overall pattern of scores corresponds with the all-India score. Therefore, it is evident that the growth of the Scheduled Castes in each of the variables of education, urbanization and industrialization, in the states as well as in the country, bears a high degree of correlation with the growth of the rest of the population in the respective variables (Table 5.17, columns 1, 2, 5, 6 and 9). There are, however, a few exceptions to this general observation. The states of Madhya Pradesh, Rajasthan and West Bengal in education (columns 1 and 2), and Andhra Pradesh and Punjab in industrialization (column 10) deviate substantially from the general pattern.

It is also evident that in the various states as well as the country, the growth of the Scheduled Castes in all the three variables bears a small degree of negative correlation with the percentage of their population in the total (columns 2, 3, 7, 8 and 10). The negative correlation, however, is more accentuated in the states of Haryana, Karnataka and Maharashtra in education (columns 3 and 4), Orissa and West Bengal in urbanization (columns 7 and 8), and Bihar, Haryana, Orissa and West Bengal (column 10) in industrialization. Wherever possible, it has already been clarified that the states markedly deviating from the general pattern are also accompanied with extraordinary features which can be linked with their exceptional showing.

Table 5.18 refers to the developmental patterns of all the three major variables brought together. First, one may call attention to a striking difference between the developmental and growth patterns. It lies in the fact that the strengths of the correlations which the variable of the growth of non-Scheduled Castes (columns 1, 2, 5, 6 and 9), and the variable of the percentage of the population of Scheduled Castes (columns 3, 4, 7, 8 and 10) bear with the developmental variables (Table 5.18) take a reverse course when compared with their correlations with the growth variables of the Scheduled Castes (Table 5.17). The correlations of the growth variables of the Scheduled Castes with the corresponding growth variables of the non-Scheduled Castes are all highly positive, but those of the developmental variables of the Scheduled Castes with the corresponding growth variables of the non-Scheduled Castes are far lower, even taking negative turns in many cases. Likewise,

Table 5.18

Scores on the Coefficients of Correlation of Each of the Developmental Variables of Education, Urbanization and Industrialization of the Scheduled Castes with the Corresponding Growth Variables of the Non-Scheduled Castes and with the Population Percentage of the Scheduled Castes in the Various States

State	I. IEE Scores Correlated with				II. IEU Scores Correlated with				III. IEI Scores Correlated with	
	% of Literate Non-SCs		% of SC Population		% of Urban Non-SCs		% of SC Population		% of Non-SC/ST NAWs	% of SC Population
	1971 (1)	1981 (2)	1971 (3)	1981 (4)	1971 (5)	1981 (6)	1971 (7)	1981 (8)	1981 (9)	1981 (10)
Andhra Pradesh	3	1	-3	-2	0	0	-1	-2	-1	-1
Bihar	1	0	-3	-3	1	0	-3	-3	0	-2
Gujarat	1	1	-2	-2	0	-1	-2	-2	0	-1
Haryana	0	2	-2	-4	-2	0	-4	-2	-1	-3
Karnataka	0	0	0	-1	0	0	-2	-2	1	-1
Kerala	3	3	0	-2	-1	0	-1	-2	1	-1
Madhya Pradesh	0	0	-2	-3	-1	-1	-2	-3	-1	0
Maharashtra	1	1	-3	-2	0	0	-3	-3	2	0
Orissa	-3	-3	-2	-1	-1	0	-2	-3	-1	-2
Punjab	2	3	0	0	-2	-3	0	0	-1	0
Rajasthan	-1	0	-2	-2	-2	-2	-1	-1	-1	0
Tamil Nadu	0	0	0	0	1	0	-1	-2	0	-2
Uttar Pradesh	2	2	-1	-2	0	0	0	-1	1	-1
West Bengal	-1	-3	0	0	-1	-2	-2	-2	-1	-3
India (states as units)	2	2	-3	-3	0	0	-3	-3	0	-1

Source: Table 5.6 for Cols. 1, 2, 3 and 4; Table 5.12 for Cols. 5, 6, 7 and 8; and Table 5.16 for Cols. 9 and 10.

the correlations of the growth variables of the Scheduled Castes with percentages of their population show a low negative value, but those of the developmental variables of the Scheduled Castes with their percentage of population assume a high negative value.

For the rest, as in the case of the growth patterns, in the case of the developmental patterns also, there is a similarity in respect of the three major variables (sets I, II and III in Table 5.18) in the basic trends. But there is some difference in the magnitude of the correlations; the scores in columns 1 and 2 are higher than their counterparts in columns 5, 6 and 9, and the scores in column 10 are lower than their counterparts in columns 3, 4, 7 and 8. The reasons for these differences have been discussed already.

The general pattern in each column (Table 5.18), by and large, conforms to the all-India score. Among the states which deviate from the general pattern, mention may be made of Orissa and West-Bengal (in columns 1 and 2), Punjab, Tamil Nadu and West Bengal (in columns 3 and 4), Haryana, Punjab, Rajasthan and West Bengal (columns 5 and 6), Punjab and Uttar Pradesh (columns 7 and 8), Maharashtra (column 9) and Haryana and West Bengal (column 10). A few of the states, particularly Punjab and West Bengal, repeat themselves in exceptions under several columns.

A few general observations may be made about the patterns of development revealed in Table 5.18. The patterns generally imply, first, that the growth of the Scheduled Castes not only does not promote the development of the Scheduled Castes but sometimes serves as a constraint. The constraining influence of this factor is very much evident in Orissa (particularly in education), Punjab (in urban and industrial development), and in Rajasthan and in West Bengal (in all the variables).

The second implication of the patterns of development is that the higher percentages of their own population are a great hurdle in the way of the development of the Scheduled Castes, which is so in most of the states. In this context it is interesting to note the states in which the population is not a constraining factor. From this point of view the state of Punjab stands out as a singularly unique instance. In none of the developmental variables of the Scheduled Castes in Punjab does their population as such seem to have restricted their development, although in the all-India context the development of the Scheduled Castes of Punjab has been greatly retarded on account of their relatively large size. In this connection it is also interesting to compare Punjab with the neighbouring state of Haryana in which the population of the Scheduled Castes has been a serious constraint on their development. Punjab and Haryana are also poles apart in many other aspects of growth and development with regard to the Scheduled Castes.

6

Development and the Scheduled Tribes

The social structure generally takes a rigid form at its extremities, especially at the bottom which, in India, is occupied by the Scheduled Castes and the Scheduled Tribes. However, as pointed out already, there are some fundamental distinctions between the two categories: whereas the Scheduled Castes are socially marginal, the Scheduled Tribes are spatially marginal. It is in recognition of these differences that the Constitution of India, while providing the Scheduled Castes and Scheduled Tribes with similar safeguards and special legal provisions for their growth and development, has kept these measures separate for the two sections commensurate with their population. It is, therefore, interesting to examine the patterns of growth and development of the Scheduled Tribes and compare them with those of the Scheduled Castes.

In analysing the growth and development of Scheduled Tribes, the same variables, data base and techniques as well as the assumptions about the social structural constraints are used, with suitable modifications, as in the study of the Scheduled Castes. The analysis in this case, however, will be on a less elaborate scale.

The Scheduled Tribes comprised 6.87, 6.82 and 7.76 per cent of India's population in 1961, 1971 and 1981* respectively, compared with the corresponding percentages of 14.70, 14.82 and 15.75 among the Scheduled Castes. Compared to the population of the Scheduled Castes, which itself is not evenly distributed, the population of the Scheduled Tribes is even more unevenly distributed in the different states of the country. Since the Scheduled Tribes usually occupy the formerly inaccessible mountainous regions, they are therefore found concentrated in the states with such

* This excludes the population of Assam.

mountainous regions which are capable of sustaining human populations. Accordingly, a large chunk of the tribal population—more than four-fifths—is spread in the mountainous terrain of the central part of the country, which extends from the southern part of West Bengal in the east to the Gujarat and Maharashtra coast in the west.

Another area where the tribal population is concentrated is the north-eastern hill areas including Assam, Arunachal Pradesh, Manipur, Meghalaya, Mizoram, Nagaland and Tripura. The tribal population of this area and of some other smaller states has been excluded from our analysis as most of these states are too small for our units and, though Assam is large enough, it does not have the relevant information for 1981. It must also be pointed out that the conclusions drawn from our analysis cannot be applied to the north-eastern region as the tribal population of this region differs markedly from that of the rest of the country in its economic, religious and educational background. Unlike the tribal population of the rest of the country, which mostly lives on the fringes of the dominant society of the plains, in the north-eastern hill areas the tribals themselves form the mainstream.

Among the larger states included in our study, Punjab and Haryana do not have any tribal population, and Kerala, Tamil Nadu and Uttar Pradesh have negligible proportions of the tribal population—about 1 per cent or less. In terms of absolute numbers, the states of Madhya Pradesh, Orissa, Bihar and Maharashtra have the four largest concentrations of Scheduled Tribe population in that descending order. In terms of the percentages of Scheduled Tribes in the total population, the states of Madhya Pradesh (22.79), Orissa (22.43), Gujarat (14.22) and Rajasthan (12.21) take the first four ranks according to the 1981 Census.

Just as the Scheduled Castes do not form a homogeneous category, so also the Scheduled Tribes are divided into a large number of tribes. However, unlike the Scheduled Castes, they are much more segregated from the rest of the population and, for the same reason, although they are economically very backward, they are not branded with the stigma of untouchability. Traditionally, the different tribes followed their own tribal religions but gradually most of them have been absorbed into Hinduism. In the 1971 Census, 87.2 per cent of the tribals have been returned as Hindus, 0.2 per cent Muslims, 6.6 per cent Christians, 0.4 per cent Buddhist and 5.6 per cent as 'Others'. The Christian tribals are found mostly in the north-eastern region and among the states included in our study, only Bihar has a substantial proportion (11 per cent in 1971) of Christians.

The study of the growth and development of the Scheduled Tribes, as in the case of the Scheduled Castes, is done through both inter-state and inter-district analyses.

Growth and Development: Inter-State Patterns

Educational Growth and Development

As already pointed out, the Scheduled Tribes are trailing behind even the Scheduled Castes in all the variables of modernization, including education. In 1961, 1971 and 1981 the percentages of literate people among them were 8.53, 11.30 and 16.35 (compared with 10.27, 14.67 and 21.38 respectively among the Scheduled Castes); the corresponding percentages in the total population as noted already were 23.98, 26.45 and 36.23.

In keeping with the trends already noticed, there are wide variations in the literacy rates of the Scheduled Tribes in the different states, the percentages ranging from 3.97 in Rajasthan to 17.26 in Kerala in 1961, from 5.34 in Andhra Pradesh to 25.72 in Kerala in 1971, and from 7.82 in Andhra Pradesh to 31.79 in Kerala in 1961; the range has widened from 13.29 in 1961 to 20.38 in 1971 and 23.97 in 1981 (Tables 6.1, 6.2 and 6.3). The phenomenon of variation is equally applicable to literacy among the non-Scheduled Tribe population also, which is similar to that of the non-Scheduled Caste population discussed already.

An interesting feature of the distribution of the percentages of literacy among the Scheduled Tribes and the non-Scheduled Tribes displayed in Tables 6.1, 6.2 and 6.3 is that whereas the ranks of the states according to the percentage of literacy are more or less constant among the non-Scheduled Tribes for 1961, 1971 and 1981, those corresponding to the percentage of literacy among the Scheduled Tribes have undergone some marked shifts from 1961 and 1971 to 1981. In 1961 and 1971 there was a greater degree of divergence between the ranks of the Scheduled Tribes and non-Scheduled Tribes; the divergence has been greatly reduced in

Table 6.1

Percentage of Literate Persons among the Scheduled Tribes
and the Rest of the Population and the Scores on the Index of Educational
Equality for the Scheduled Tribes in the Larger States of India (1961)

State	% of Literate among STs		% of Literate among Non-STs		IEE	
	% (1)	Rank (2)	% (3)	Rank (4)	Score (5)	Rank (6)
Andhra Pradesh	4.41	10	21.84	8	20	10
Bihar	9.16	3	19.32	10	47	1
Gujarat	11.69	2	33.34	2	35	3
Karnataka	8.15	4	25.54	7	32	4
Kerala	17.26	1	47.24	1	37	2
Madhya Pradesh	5.10	9	20.25	9	25	6
Maharashtra	7.21	6	31.27	4	23	8
Orissa	7.36	5	26.19	6	28	5
Rajasthan	3.97	11	16.69	11	24	7
Tamil Nadu	5.91	8	31.60	3	19	11
West Bengal	6.55	7	30.70	5	21	9
India	8.53	—	25.10	—	34	—

Source: *Census of India*, 1961, General Population Tables, and Special Tables for Scheduled Tribes.

1981. Accordingly, the Rank Difference coefficients of correlation between the ranks of the Scheduled Tribes and the non-Scheduled Tribes in 1961, 1971 and 1981 are 0.563, 0.455 and 0.734 respectively. In other words, there is an increasing tendency for the growth of the Scheduled Tribes in education to be correlated with that of the non-Scheduled Tribes.

However, even in 1981 the degree of correlation in literacy between the Scheduled Tribes and the non-Scheduled Tribes was substantially lower than that between the Scheduled Castes and the non-Scheduled Castes (0.916). This is because the Scheduled Castes are much ahead of the Scheduled Tribes in literacy. There are indications that with further advancement the Scheduled Tribes will catch up with the Scheduled Castes in this respect.

In every state the literacy level of the Scheduled Tribes is far lower than that of the non-Scheduled Tribes. The IEE scores of the Scheduled Tribes shown in column 5 of Tables 6.1, 6.2 and 6.3 (which stand for the educational development of the Scheduled Tribes) also show a wide variation from state to state, ranging

Table 6.2

Percentage of Literate Persons among the Scheduled Tribes
and the Rest of the Population and the Scores on the Index of Educational
Equality for the Scheduled Tribes in the Larger States of India (1971)

State	% of Literate among STs		% of Literate among Non-STs		IEE	
	% (1)	Rank (2)	% (3)	Rank (4)	Score. (5)	Rank (6)
Andhra Pradesh	5.34	12	25.51	9	21	12
Bihar	11.64	6	21.72	11	54	2
Gujarat	14.12	4	41.37	3	34	5
Karnataka	14.85	2	31.75	7	47	3
Kerala	25.72	1	61.17	1	42	4
Madhya Pradesh	7.62	10	27.63	8	28	9
Maharashtra	11.74	5	41.55	2	28	7
Orissa	9.46	7	33.89	6	28	8
Rajasthan	6.47	11	21.65	12	30	6
Tamil Nadu	9.02	8	39.75	4	23	11
Uttar Pradesh	14.59	3	21.75	10	67	1
West Bengal	8.92	9	35.18	5	25	10
India	11.30		34.15		33	

Source: *Census of India*, 1971, Union Primary Census Abstract, and Special Tables
for Scheduled Tribes.

from 19 in Tamil Nadu to 47 in Bihar in 1961, from 21 in Andhra
Pradesh to 67 in Uttar Pradesh in 1971 and from 25 to 75 in the
same states in 1981. The range has widened from 28 in 1961 to 46
and 50 in 1971 and 1981. Thus in both educational growth and
development of the Scheduled Tribes, the inequalities between the
states at the top and at the bottom of the hierarchy have widened.
Obviously, these trends are similar to the ones noticed in the case
of the Scheduled Castes.

There is a high degree of correlation (although to a lesser extent
when compared with the Scheduled Castes in a similar situation)
between the IEE scores and the percentage of literacy of the
Scheduled Tribes, the coefficients of correlation being 0.782, 0.745
and 0.650 in 1961, 1971 and 1981 respectively. The decline of the
strength of the correlation from 1961 through 1981 is in conformity
with a similar trend among the Scheduled Castes.

However, when we come to the correlation between the IEE
scores of the Scheduled Tribes and the percentage of literacy
among the non-Scheduled Tribes, the situation takes a very different

Table 6.3
Percentage of Literate Persons among the Scheduled Tribes
and the Rest of the Population and the Scores on the Index of Educational
Equality for the Scheduled Tribes in the Larger States of India (1981)

State	% of Literate among STs		% of Literate among Non-STs		IEE	
	% (1)	Rank (2)	% (3)	Rank (4)	Score (5)	Rank (6)
Andhra Pradesh	7.82	12	31.34	9	25	12
Bihar	16.99	7	27.04	11	63	2
Gujarat	21.14	3	47.44	3	45	6
Karnataka	20.14	6	39.41	7	51	3
Kerala	31.79	1	70.82	1	45	4
Madhya Pradesh	10.68	10	33.00	8	32	10
Maharashtra	22.29	2	49.70	2	45	5
Orissa	13.96	8	40.10	6	35	9
Rajasthan	10.27	11	26.35	12	39	8
Tamil Nadu	20.46	4	47.05	4	43	7
Uttar Pradesh	20.45	5	27.17	10	75	1
West Bengal	13.21	9	42.59	5	31	11
India	16.35		37.90		43	

Source: *Census of India*, 1981, Primary Census Abstract, General Population, and Scheduled Tribes.

turn; whereas there is a moderate degree of correlation in the case of the Scheduled Castes, in the case of the Scheduled Tribes it is negligible or nil, being 0.009, −0.189 and −0.007 in 1961, 1971 and 1981 respectively. Thus the educational advancement of a state has hardly any impact on the educational development of the Scheduled Tribes.

In other words, the relationships of the percentage of literacy among the non-Scheduled Tribes with the percentage of literacy among the Scheduled Tribes and with the IEE scores of the Scheduled Tribes follow different patterns, which is true in the case of the Scheduled Castes also. On the whole, the broad trends of the growth and development of the Scheduled Tribes in education are similar to the ones noticed in the case of the Scheduled Castes.

Urban Growth and Development

The relatively high degree of segregation of the Scheduled Tribes from the rest of the population is reflected in their exceedingly low degree of representation in urban areas. Only 2.59, 3.41 and 6.20 per cent of the Scheduled Tribes were found in the urban areas in 1961, 1971 and 1981 respectively; they compare with the corresponding percentages of 10.70, 11.94 and 16.00 among the Scheduled Castes and 17.95, 19.96 and 23.31 in the total population.

Urbanization of the Scheduled Tribes in the various states (Tables 6.4, 6.5 and 6.6) is highly variable, ranging from 1.12 in Madhya Pradesh to 5.66 in Tamil Nadu in 1961, from 1.71 in Madhya Pradesh to 10.90 in Karnataka in 1971, and from 1.91 in Kerala to 12.87 in Karnataka in 1981, the range having been widened from 4.54 to 9.19 and 10.6 over the decades. In two states, Kerala and Uttar Pradesh, the percentage has declined from 1971 to 1981, which is a rather rare phenomenon. But these are states with a negligible Scheduled Tribe population.

Table 6.4

Percentage of Urban Population among the Scheduled Tribes and Non-Scheduled Tribes and the Scores on the Index of Urban Equality for the Scheduled Tribes in the Larger States of India (1961)

State	% of Urban among STs		% of Urban among Non-STs		IEU	
	% (1)	Rank (2)	% (3)	Rank (4)	Score (5)	Rank (6)
Andhra Pradesh	4.31	4	17.94	7	24	4
Bihar	2.61	7	9.00	10	29	1
Gujarat	5.01	3	28.96	2	17	7
Karnataka	5.13	2	22.47	5	23	5
Kerala	3.94	5	15.25	9	26	2
Madhya Pradesh	1.12	11	17.71	8	6	11
Maharashtra	3.75	6	29.80	1	13	8
Orissa	2.07	9	7.67	11	27	3
Rajasthan	2.01	10	18.16	6	11	9
Tamil Nadu	5.66	1	26.85	3	21	6
West Bengal	2.33	8	25.84	4	9	10
India	2.59	—	19.07	—	14	—

Source: *Census of India*, 1961, General Population Tables, and Special Tables for Scheduled Tribes.

There is a low to moderate degree of correlation between the urbanization of the Scheduled Tribes and that of the non-Scheduled Tribes, the coefficients of correlation being 0.463, 0.206 and 0.524

Table 6.5

*Percentage of Urban Population among the Scheduled Tribes
and Non-Scheduled Tribes and the Scores on the Index of Urban Equality
for the Scheduled Tribes in the Larger States of India (1971)*

State	% of Urban among STs		% of Urban among Non-STs		IEU	
	% (1)	Rank (2)	% (3)	Rank (4)	Score (5)	Rank (6)
Andhra Pradesh	5.13	5	19.88	7	26	5
Bihar	4.20	7	10.55	11	40	3
Gujarat	6.09	3	31.66	2	19	7
Karnataka	10.90	1	24.42	5	45	2
Kerala	4.04	8	16.39	9	25	6
Madhya Pradesh	1.71	12	19.96	6	9	12
Maharashtra	4.34	6	32.84	1	13	9
Orissa	2.91	9	10.06	12	29	4
Rajasthan	2.17	11	19.77	8	11	10
Tamil Nadu	5.50	4	30.44	3	18	8
Uttar Pradesh	7.96	2	14.04	10	57	1
West Bengal	2.26	10	26.11	4	9	11
India	3.41	—	21.62	—	16	—

Source: *Census of India*, 1971, Union Primary Census Abstract, and Special Tables
for Scheduled Tribes.

in 1961, 1971 and 1981 respectively. These coefficients are much
smaller than those between the literacy of the Scheduled Tribes
and that of the non-Scheduled Tribes (0.563, 0.455 and 0.734
respectively). But the two sets of correlations are similar in the
sense that in both the cases, their degrees have decreased from
1961 to 1971 but have sharply increased from 1971 to 1981.

As regards the finding that the degrees of the particular correlations in respect to the urbanization of the Scheduled Tribes are
smaller than of those in respect to their education, we also noticed
a similar finding in the case of the Scheduled Castes.

The urban development of the Scheduled Tribes, which is
indicated by their IEU scores (Tables 6.4, 6.5 and 6.6, column 5),
is very low for the total Scheduled Tribe population, the scores
being 14, 16 and 25 in 1961, 1971 and 1981 respectively. The IEU
scores are below 100 in every state, and in some states (such as
Madhya Pradesh and West Bengal) they are abysmally low. The
variation in the IEU scores is very high, ranging from 6 in Madhya

Table 6.6

Percentage of Urban Population among the Scheduled Tribes
and Non-Scheduled Tribes and the Scores on the Index of Urban Equality
for the Scheduled Tribes in the Larger States of India (1981)

State	% of Urban among STs		% of Urban among Non-STs		IEU	
	% (1)	Rank (2)	% (3)	Rank (4)	Score (5)	Rank (6)
Andhra Pradesh	6.22	6	24.40	7	25	7
Bihar	6.23	5	13.04	12	48	1
Gujarat	7.32	4	35.05	2	21	8
Karnataka	12.87	1	29.72	4	43	2
Kerala	1.91	12	18.92	9	10	12
Madhya Pradesh	3.62	11	25.26	6	14	10
Maharashtra	10.43	2	37.52	1	28	5
Orissa	4.60	8	13.87	11	33	3
Rajasthan	3.73	10	23.45	8	16	9
Tamil Nadu	9.69	3	33.20	3	29	4
Uttar Pradesh	4.72	7	17.98	10	26	6
West Bengal	3.76	9	27.82	5	14	11
India	6.39	—	25.17	—	25	—

Source: *Census of India*, 1981, Primary Census Abstract, General Population, and
Scheduled Tribes.

Pradesh to 29 in Bihar in 1961, from 9 in Madhya Pradesh and
West Bengal to 57 in Uttar Pradesh in 1971 and from 10 in Madhya
Pradesh to 48 in Bihar in 1981. Although the range has come down
from 48 to 38 from 1971 to 1981, this is due to the uncommon
phenomenon of regression in urbanization in Uttar Pradesh. But
for this aberration, the oft-repeated observation about the growing
inequalities in the development of the Scheduled Castes or Tribes
between the states which are at the top and the bottom of a
variable are evident in this case also.

As expected, there is a correlation between the growth (percentage of urban population) and development (IEU scores) of
the Scheduled Tribes, the coefficients of correlation being 0.364,
0.685 and 0.734 in 1961, 1971 and 1981 respectively; the strength
of the correlation has increased over the decades. These correlations are stronger than the corresponding coefficients for the
Scheduled Castes (0.484, 0.413 and 0.409 respectively).

It is interesting to note that in 1961 and 1971, there was a moderate degree of negative correlation between the IEU scores of the Scheduled Tribes and the percentage of urban population of the non-Scheduled Tribes (r = −0.545 and −0.518 respectively), but the degree of the correlation had come down to −0.119 in 1981. This trend would indicate that in the earlier phases of urbanization of a state, the gap between the Scheduled Tribes and the non-Scheduled Tribes was widening. Such a tendency has now been checked and the urban development of the Scheduled Tribes is becoming independent of the urbanization of the state—a situation which is close to that of the Scheduled Castes in this respect. Further, it has been observed in the case of the Scheduled Castes that there is a correlation between their scores in the IEE and IEU, which is also true in the case of the Scheduled Tribes, the relevant coefficients of correlation in 1961, 1971 and 1981 being 0.491, 0.601 and 0.612 respectively. These correlations in the case of the Scheduled Tribes are even higher than the corresponding correlations in the case of the Scheduled Castes (0.434, 0.314 and 0.448 in 1961, 1971 and 1981 respectively).

Industrial Growth and Development

As mentioned earlier while dealing with the Scheduled Castes, the percentage of non-agricultural occupations has been employed as an index of industrialization. However, at an earlier point of time, especially in 1961, the percentage of non-agricultural occupations was not a satisfactory index of modernization as the share of the occupations in the organized sector was too low. Therefore, even though in 1961 the Scheduled Tribes had a relatively high percentage (12.11) of non-agricultural occupations (compared with 7.53 and 12.90 in 1971 and 1981 respectively), it does not indicate their level of modernization in 1961 (Tables 6.7, 6.8 and 6.9). These percentages compare with the corresponding percentages of 22.39, 13.63 and 23.61 among the Scheduled Castes in 1961, 1971 and 1981 respectively. Both among the Scheduled Tribes and Castes there has been a sharp decline in the percentage of non-agricultural occupations from 1961 to 1971 and an equally remarkable increase from 1971 to 1981. This change corresponds with the sudden fall in the percentage of occupations classified under household industries from 1961 to 1971.

The variation in the percentages of the non-agricultural workers

Table 6.7

*Percentage of Non-Agricultural Workers among the Scheduled Tribes
and Non-Scheduled Tribes and the Scores on the Index of Equality
of Industrialization for the Scheduled Tribes in the Larger States of India (1961)*

State	Non-Agricultural Workers among STs		Non-Agricultural Workers among Non-STs		IEI of STs	
	% (1)	Rank (2)	% (3)	Rank (4)	Score (5)	Rank (6)
Andhra Pradesh	17.69	5	31.91	5	55	2
Bihar	12.34	7	24.76	10	50	6
Gujarat	9.78	9	36.58	4	27	11
Karnataka	27.02	2	29.47	8	92	1
Kerala	32.93	1	62.22	1	53	4
Madhya Pradesh	7.13	11	24.97	9	29	10
Maharashtra	10.07	8	31.70	6	32	9
Orissa	16.29	6	30.34	7	54	3
Rajasthan	8.93	10	24.43	11	37	8
Tamil Nadu	20.98	4	39.68	3	53	5
West Bengal	22.85	3	48.48	2	47	7
India	12.11	—	32.29	—	38	—

Source: *Census of India*, 1961, General Population Tables, and Special Tables for
Scheduled Tribes.

(NAWs) among the Scheduled Tribes in the different states is very
considerable, ranging from 7.13 in Madhya Pradesh to 32.93 in
Kerala in 1961, from 3.67 in Madhya Pradesh to 25.01 in Karnataka
in 1971, and from 7.79 in Madhya Pradesh to 21.99 in Kerala
(Tables 6.7, 6.8 and 6.9, column 1). The range has come down
from 25.80 in 1961 and 21.34 in 1971 to 14.20 in 1981. The steady
decrease in the range should not be interpreted as an improvement
in the inter-state equity in the industrial growth of the Scheduled
Tribes. It may have something to do with the decline in the
percentage of non-agricultural occupations from 1961 to 1971 and
with the minor definitional changes in the list of Scheduled Tribes
as a result of which there has been a sudden increase in the
Scheduled Tribe population of Karnataka and Maharashtra. It is
obvious that as a result of new people joining the ranks of the
Scheduled Tribes of Karnataka in 1981, it has lost its prominent
position in the percentage of non-agricultural workers. The percentage has actually come down from 25.01 in 1971 to 18.46 in

Table 6.8

*Percentage of Non-Agricultural Workers among the Scheduled Tribes
and Non-Scheduled Tribes and the Scores on the Index of Equality
of Industrialization for the Scheduled Tribes in the Larger States of India (1971)*

State	Non-Agricultural Workers among STs		Non-Agricultural Workers among Non-STs		IEI of STs	
	% (1)	Rank (2)	% (3)	Rank (4)	Score (5)	Rank (6)
Andhra Pradesh	12.48	5	30.65	7	41	3
Bihar	7.43	8	18.82	12	39	4
Gujarat	5.81	9	40.22	8	14	11
Karnataka	25.01	1	33.36	6	75	1
Kerala	18.27	3	52.09	1	35	7
Madhya Pradesh	3.67	12	25.20	10	15	10
Maharashtra	4.95	11	37.45	5	13	12
Orissa	9.21	6	27.00	9	34	8
Rajasthan	5.73	10	28.62	8	20	9
Tamil Nadu	15.04	4	38.49	4	39	4
Uttar Pradesh	8.66	7	22.04	11	39	4
West Bengal	18.79	2	43.42	2	43	2
India	7.53	—	32.27	—	23	—

Source: *Census of India*, 1971, Union Primary Census Abstract, and Special Tables
for Scheduled Tribes.

1981, which is really uncommon. On the other hand, a rise in the
tribal population of Maharashtra as a result of definitional changes
has resulted in the equally uncommon experience of a steep rise in
its percentage of non-agricultural workers among the Scheduled
Tribes from 4.95 in 1971 to 15.25 in 1981.

The industrial growth of the Scheduled Tribes (Tables 6.7, 6.8
and 6.9, column 5) is correlated to a moderate to a high degree
with the growth of industrialization of the non-Scheduled Tribes
(column 6), the coefficients of correlation being 0.627, 0.574 and
0.671 in 1961, 1971 and 1981 respectively; this follows a similar
pattern in the industrial growth of the Scheduled Castes (the corresponding coefficients of correlation being 0.560, 0.494 and 0.617).

The scores on the index of equality of industrialization of the
Scheduled Tribes have shown a zig-zag course from 38 in 1961 to
23 in 1971 and 36 in 1981, which is consistent with the changes in
the percentage of non-agricultural workers. In spite of the relatively

Table 6.9
Percentage of Non-Agricultural Workers among the Scheduled Tribes
and Non-Scheduled Tribes and the Scores on the Index of Equality
of Industrialization for the Scheduled Tribes in the Larger States of India (1981)

State	Non-Agricultural Workers among STs		Non-Agricultural Workers among Non-STs		IEI of STs	
	% (1)	Rank (2)	% (3)	Rank (4)	Score (5)	Rank (6)
Andhra Pradesh	13.07	9	31.77	8	41	6
Bihar	13.74	8	21.77	12	63	1
Gujarat	13.96	7	45.54	2	31	11
Karnataka	14.46	4	35.98	6	51	3
Kerala	21.99	1	58.70	1	37	8
Madhya Pradesh	7.79	12	29.92	10	26	12
Maharashtra	15.25	5	41.20	4	37	8
Orissa	11.64	11	30.42	9	38	7
Rajasthan	12.08	10	33.90	7	36	10
Tamil Nadu	18.74	3	39.32	5	48	4
Uttar Pradesh	14.04	6	25.53	11	55	2
West Bengal	20.23	2	44.72	3	45	5
India	12.90		35.74		36	

Source: *Census of India*, 1981, Primary Census Abstract, General Population
Tables, and for Scheduled Tribes.

rapid changes, the Scheduled Tribes are way behind the Scheduled
Castes (IEI score = 66 in 1981) let alone the non-Scheduled Tribes.
With regard to the IEI scores of the Scheduled Tribes also, there is
wide variation in the states, ranging from 27 in Gujarat to 92 in
Karnataka in 1961, from 13 in Maharashtra to 75 in Karnataka in
1971, and from 26 in Madhya Pradesh to 63 in Bihar in 1981. The
decline in the range in this case also is spurious as in the case of the
percentage of non-agricultural workers among the Scheduled
Tribes for the same reasons discussed already.

The industrial development of the Scheduled Tribes (IEI scores)
was highly correlated with their industrial growth in 1961 and 1971
with coefficients of correlation of 0.745 and 0.803 respectively.
However, with the spurt in industrialization as well as sudden
increases in the tribal populations of Karnataka and Maharashtra,
this correlation has declined to a moderate level of 0.526 in 1981.

On the other hand, it bears hardly any correlation with the industrial growth of the non-Scheduled Tribes in 1961 and 1971 ($r = 0.136$ and 0.011 respectively) and even a moderate degree of negative correlation (-0.417) in 1981. In other words, the industrial growth of a state, in general, worsens the inter-state equity in the industrial development of the Scheduled Tribes. In the case of the Scheduled Castes also, there is a similar tendency noticeable but it is very weak and declining, the corresponding coefficients of correlation in 1961, 1971 and 1981 being -0.439, -0.345 and -0.189 respectively.

Since industrialization in general is highly correlated with the per capita domestic product (PCDP), as already discussed in Chapter 3, it would be interesting to examine how the industrial growth and development of the Scheduled Tribes have reacted to it. So far as the industrial growth of the Scheduled Tribes is concerned, it bore a low degree of positive correlation with the PCDP in 1961 and 1971 (0.209 and 0.203 respectively) but the degree of correlation had increased substantially (0.565) in 1981. However, the correlation of the IEI scores or the development of the Scheduled Tribes with the PCDP was negative in all the years, the values of the coefficients being -0.428, -0.213 and -0.255 respectively in 1961, 1971 and 1981.

At this stage, when we have a comparative view of the growth and development of the Scheduled Tribes in all the three variables of modernization (namely, education, urbanization and industrialization), we may identify some general features. The Scheduled Tribes have advanced in all the three variables from 1961 to 1981 (except industrialization from 1961 to 1971) both in an absolute sense and in a relative sense in comparison with the non-Scheduled Tribes. But the inter-state growth and development have been highly inequitable. The inequity in growth, however, can be largely attributed to the general process of growth itself, although it does not account for it fully; with the advancement in modernization, the inequalities of the Scheduled Tribes in the different states have increased. But the modernization process does not account for the growing inequalities in development in the different variables. Therefore, for a fuller understanding of this problem we have to turn to the structural variables as represented by the population percentages of the Scheduled Tribes and Castes.

The Structural Variables

In Chapter 4, it was explained how structural forces channel the economic opportunities for the Scheduled Castes and how the percentages of the populations of the Scheduled Castes and Tribes can be taken as the proxies for some kind of structural forces. With suitable modifications, the same kind of explanation about the operation of structural forces in their mobility opportunities may hold good in the case of the Scheduled Tribes also. It is generally true that the Scheduled Tribes are much more backward than the Scheduled Castes in the variables of modernization. While it is true that when the Scheduled Tribes are under-represented and the Scheduled Castes are over-represented, the former may have an edge over the latter, the advantage in their case may be smaller than in the case of the Scheduled Castes in a similar context.

We may, therefore, formulate the structural hypotheses about the mobility opportunities of the Scheduled Tribes as follows: First, the larger the percentage of the Scheduled Tribes in a state, the lower are their chances of upward mobility and, second, the higher the percentage of Scheduled Castes in a state the better are the chances of the mobility of the Scheduled Tribes. The force of the second hypothesis, however, is weakened because of the fact that the Scheduled Tribes are generally more backward than the Scheduled Castes.

Let us first consider to what extent the structural factors are an impediment to the growth of the Scheduled Tribes in the variables of modernization. The coefficients of correlation of each of the variables of growth—percentage of literacy, percentage of urban population and percentage of non-agricultural workers—with the percentage of the Scheduled Tribe population and with the percentage of the Scheduled Caste population are given in Table 6.10 for the years 1961, 1971 and 1981. It was observed in the case of the Scheduled Castes that although the structural variables exerted an influence over their growth in the variables of modernization, the effect was not much; secondly, the effect of the percentage of their own population was negative and that of the other category (Scheduled Tribes) was positive. In the case of the Scheduled Tribes, however, the pattern is not as clear. First of all, the size of their own population has seriously hampered their growth in urbanization and industrialization. In urbanization, however, the influence of the size of the population has suddenly declined in 1981. On the other hand, although the negative effect of the size of their population is small on the growth of education, it has increased over the decades.

Table 6.10

Coefficients of Correlation between the Growth Variables of the Scheduled Tribes and the Structural Variables in 1961, 1971 and 1981

Growth Variable (Percentage)	Structural Variables					
	% of ST Population			% of SC Population		
	1961 (1)	1971 (2)	1981 (3)	1961 (4)	1971 (5)	1981 (6)
Literate	−0.054	−0.363	−0.385	−0.455	−0.301	−0.426
Urban	−0.744	−0.649	−0.133	−0.188	−0.042	−0.077
Non-agricultural workers	−0.764	−0.594	−0.776	0.209	−0.322	0.100

Source: *Census of India*, 1961, 1971, and 1981, Tables for General Population, for Scheduled Castes, and for Scheduled Tribes.

The values of the coefficients of correlation between the growth variables of the Scheduled Tribes and the size of the Scheduled Caste population were expected to be small but positive. As expected, it is small, but unexpectedly they are mostly negative. Only in the case of industrialization (percentage of non-agricultural workers) are two values out of three in the expected direction. The negative correlation between the population percentage of the Scheduled Castes and the growth in modernization of the Scheduled Tribes generally agrees with the relative superiority of the Scheduled Castes; whereas the larger size of the Scheduled Castes should prove an advantage to the Scheduled Tribes in their modernization, the relative superiority of the former would act as a disadvantage.

The coefficients of correlation between the developmental variables (index of equality scores) and the structural variables are given in Table 6.11. Here, also, the pattern is not so striking as in the case of the Scheduled Castes. Only in the case of industrial development (IEI) are our hypotheses fully confirmed. As expected, the IEI scores are moderately correlated in a negative way with the percentage of their own (Scheduled Tribes) population;

they are positively related with the percentage of the population of the Scheduled Castes. For the rest the evidence is not quite conclusive. Thus, the structural factors can be seen to be most at work in the case of the industrial development of the Scheduled Tribes.

Table 6.11

Coefficients of Correlation between the Developmental Variables of the Scheduled Tribes and the Structural Variables in 1961, 1971 and 1981

Developmental Variable	Structural Variables					
	% of ST Population			% of SC Population		
	1961 (1)	1971 (2)	1981 (3)	1961 (4)	1971 (5)	1981 (6)
IEE scores	−0.300	−0.175	−0.468	−0.409	−0.063	−0.133
IEU scores	−0.227	−0.365	−0.007	−0.064	0.154	−0.021
IEI scores	−0.527	−0.640	−0.670	0.281	0.586	0.521

Source: *Census of India*, 1961, 1971 and 1981, Tables for General Population, for Scheduled Castes, and for Scheduled Tribes.

It has been pointed out that the patterns of relationships between the structural variables and the developmental variables are much clearer and sharper in the case of the Scheduled Castes. However, the Scheduled Castes are far more advanced than the Scheduled Tribes. It is possible that the influence of the structural factors becomes stronger with a greater degree of development which also generates greater competition. Therefore, while noting the differences between the Scheduled Tribes and Castes in their growth and developmental patterns, one may recognize that more or less the same socio-economic forces are at work in both the sets of patterns.

Evidence about School Enrolment

As in the case of the Scheduled Castes, let us consider some of the evidence about school enrolment of the Scheduled Tribes also. The relevant information is presented in Table 6.12 which gives the scores on the coefficient of equality in enrolment for the Scheduled Tribes separately for all schools together and for the

Table 6.12

Coefficients of Equality in Enrolment for the Scheduled Tribes by Type of Institution in Selected States in 1960–61, 1970–71 and 1980–81

State	All Institutions						High/Higher Secondary					
	1960–61		1970–71		1980–81		1960–61		1970–71		1980–81	
	Score	Rank	Score	Rank	Score	Rank	Score	Rank	Score	Rank	Score	Rank
Andhra Pradesh	47	5	55	2	75	4	16	3	19	6	54	2
Bihar	77	1	82	1	102	1	35	1	44	1	66	1
Gujarat	57	2	54	3	78	2	12	5	19	6	36	4
Madhya Pradesh	38	6	46	6	57	7	8	7	19	6	29	6
Maharashtra	56	3	53	4	62	6	16	3	34	2	29	6
Orissa	30	7	47	5	76	3	10	6	20	4	33	5
Rajasthan	13	8	43	7	70	5	4	8	21	3	47	3
West Bengal	53	4	42	8	54	8	19	2	20	4	22	8
India	54	—	55	—	71	—	15	—	24	—	43	—

Source: K.C. Nautiyal and Y.D. Sharma, *Equalization of Educational Opportunities for Scheduled Castes and Scheduled Tribes*, New Delhi, NCERT, 1978; Government of India, *Statewise Information on Education of Scheduled Castes and Scheduled Tribes*, New Delhi, Ministry of Education, 1985.

High/Higher Secondary schools for the years 1960–61, 1970–71 and 1980–81. As expected, the coefficient of equality (CE) scores are much higher in total enrolment as compared to those in enrolment to High/Higher Secondary schools; however, the ratio between the two sets has been improving over the years.

There is also a broad agreement between the ranks of the states on the CE scores over the three points of time with certain significant changes. The state of Bihar has always stood at the top of the hierarchy. Maharashtra and West Bengal have shown a continual decline whereas Orissa and Rajasthan have maintained a steady improvement in their ranks over the years. The state of Andhra Pradesh presents a fluctuating picture in this respect.

The enrolment pattern of the Scheduled Tribes in the different states cannot be satisfactorily explained in terms of the structural or the economic growth factors. This has been found to be so even in the case of the pattern of IEE score. But it is interesting to observe that the correspondence between the ranks on the CE scores and the IEE scores has increased over the years, the coefficients of correlation between the two sets of ranks being 0.333, 0.357 and 0.524 in 1960–61, 1970–71 and 1980–81 respectively. It may be suggested that the interaction between the relevant factors would intensify as the volume of enrolment grows.

Development of the Scheduled Tribes Compared with Regional Growth and Structural Factors

As in the case of the Scheduled Castes, it would be useful to examine the influence of the structural factors on the development of the Scheduled Tribes in each state by comparing their developmental variables on the one hand, with the percentages of the population of the Scheduled Tribes and Castes on the other.

It has been observed that in the case of the Scheduled Tribes the influence of the structural factors has so far crystallized to an appreciable extent mainly in the case of industrial development. Therefore, in Table 6.13 the relevant data are presented only in respect of the industrial development of the Scheduled Tribes. The ranking of the states on the IEI scores of the Scheduled Tribes is compared with their ranking on the percentage of non-agricultural

Table 6.13

Industrial Development of the Scheduled Tribes Compared with the Industrialization of the Non-Scheduled Tribes and with the Population Percentage of the Scheduled Castes and Tribes in 1961, 1971 and 1981

State	Ranking on Percentage of Non-Agricultural Workers among Non-STs			Ranking on IEI Scores of the STs			Ranking* on the 1971 Percentage of Population of			
	1961 (1)	1971 (2)	1981 (3)	1961 (4)	1971 (5)	1981 (6)	STs (7)		SCs (8)	
Andhra Pradesh	5	7	8	2	3	6	8	M*	7	M*
Bihar	10	12	12	6	4	1	5	M	6	M
Gujarat	4	8	2	11	11	11	3	H	11	L
Karnataka	8	6	6	1	1	3	10	L	8	M
Kerala	1	1	1	4	7	8	9	L	10	L
Madhya Pradesh	9	10	10	10	10	12	2	H	9	L
Maharashtra	6	5	4	9	12	8	6	M	12	L
Orissa	7	9	9	3	8	7	1	H	5	M
Rajasthan	11	8	7	8	9	10	4	H	4	H
Tamil Nadu	3	4	5	5	4	4	11	L	3	H
Uttar Pradesh	—	11	11	—	4	2	12	L	1	H
West Bengal	2	2	3	7	2	5	7	M	2	H

Source: Table 6.7 for Cols. 1 and 4; Table 6.8 for Cols. 2 and 5; Table 6.9 for Cols. 3 and 6; and Table 4.19 for Cols. 7 and 8.
* H = high (ranks 1, 2, 3 & 4); M = medium (ranks 5, 6, 7 & 8);
L = low (ranks 9, 10, 11 & 12).
Note: Ranks of the States in the different variables are compared.

workers among the non-Scheduled Tribes and with the ranking on the percentages of the populations of the Scheduled Tribes and Castes. Since the population percentages of these sections are more or less stable over the years, the information on these variables pertains to only 1971 whereas the other variables refer to three points of time—1961, 1971 and 1981. It may, however, be pointed out that because of some minor definitional changes there is slight difference in the ranks of the states on the percentage of Scheduled Tribe population in 1971 and 1981.

The assessment regarding the influence of the structural factors on the industrial development of the Scheduled Tribes may be made on two assumptions. First, for an equitable developmental situation of the Scheduled Tribes, the rank of a state on the IEI score (say, column 4 in Table 6.13) should correspond with its rank on the growth of the non-Scheduled Tribes in the relevant variable (column 1). Second, the difference between the two ranks, if any, should be consistent with the structural factors (columns 7 or 8 or both); a higher rank in the development of the Scheduled Tribes in relation to the rank on the growth of the non-Scheduled Tribes should be accompanied with a lower rank on the percentage of the population of the Scheduled Tribes or a higher rank on the percentage of the population of the Scheduled Castes or both; the relatively lower rank on the developmental variable should be accompanied with the opposite set of conditions. If the structural factors cannot account for the difference, then the operation of some other factor or factors has to be posited.

An examination of Table 6.13 reveals that if we ignore the difference of one step between any two ranks in a state, the ranks of the states on the variable of the industrial growth of the non-Scheduled Tribes (columns 1, 2 and 3) or of the industrial development of the Scheduled Tribes (columns 4, 5 and 6) are more or less stable over the three points of time—1961, 1971 and 1981. The coefficients of correlation between the ranks in columns 1 and 2 and between columns 2 and 3 are 0.817 and 0.858; those between the ranks in columns 4 and 5, and between columns 5 and 6 are 0.724 and 0.802 respectively. This would mean that the rank orders between the years 1971 and 1981 in each of the sets of variables are relatively more stable than the rank orders in the corresponding variables between the years of 1961 and 1971. It may be recalled that the percentage of non-agricultural occupations in 1961 as an index of modernization was less satisfactory than during the subsequent years. The coefficients of correlation also indicate that the ranks on the industrial growth of the non-Scheduled Tribes were slightly more stable than the ranks on the industrial development of the Scheduled Tribes.

Another fact which emerges from Table 6.13 is that in most cases the ranks on the industrial growth of the non-Scheduled Tribes (columns 1, 2 and 3) in any state are radically different from those on the industrial development of the Scheduled Tribes (columns 4, 5, and 6). In other words, there is no agreement between the ranks on the industrial growth of the non-Scheduled Tribes and the industrial development of the Scheduled Tribes. On this basis most of the states can be divided into two categories: (*a*) the states in which the industrial development of the Scheduled Tribes is better than the industrial growth of the non-Scheduled Tribes, and (b) the states in which the industrial development of the Scheduled Tribes is worse than the industrial growth of the non-Scheduled Tribes. The first group includes the states of Andhra Pradesh, Bihar, Karnataka, Orissa, Tamil Nadu and Uttar Pradesh; the second encompasses the states of Gujarat, Kerala, Madhya Pradesh, Maharashtra, Rajasthan and West Bengal. In the classification of Rajasthan and Tamil Nadu, the situation in 1961 has been ignored.

For the convenience of reconciling the different types of developmental categories with the different structural patterns, the ranks on the percentages of the Scheduled Tribe and Caste population can be divided into three broad rubrics—high ranks (including positions 1, 2, 3 and 4), medium ranks (including positions 5, 6, 7 and 8), and low ranks (including positions 9, 10, 11 and 12). Where the development of the Scheduled Tribes is higher than the growth of the non-Scheduled Tribes (states in category a), the structural situation of the states, ideally speaking, should be characterized by a low rank on the percentage of Scheduled Tribe population and a high rank on the percentage of Scheduled Caste population; the combination of high and low is totally inconsistent. On the other hand, where the development of the Scheduled Tribes is lower than the growth of the non-Scheduled Tribes (states in category b), the ideal-typical structural situation should be represented by a high rank on the Scheduled Tribe population and a low rank on the Scheduled Caste population; the combination of low and high, in this case is totally inconsistent.

When we examine the pattern of ranks on the percentages of the Scheduled Tribe and Caste populations according to the two categories of states, a and b, we find that first of all there is not a single state in which any of the totally inconsistent combinations of the ranks is found. There are, however, other less inconsistent combinations. In the states included in category a, the combination of ranks on the Scheduled Tribe and Caste populations are *low-high* (Tamil Nadu and Uttar Pradesh), *low-medium* (Karnataka) and *medium-medium* (Andhra Pradesh and Bihar). All these combinations are acceptable as satisfactory structural explanations. Only one combination, *high-medium*, in the case of Orissa seems to be out of character with our explanation. In category b states, the acceptable combinations are *high-low* (Gujarat and Madhya

Pradesh), and *medium-low* (Maharashtra). Other less acceptable combinations are *high-high* (Rajasthan), *medium-high* (West Bengal) and *low-low* (Kerala); what makes them less acceptable is the high rank on the population of Scheduled Castes in Rajasthan and the low rank on the population of the Scheduled Tribes in Kerala. However, in all these three states one of the complementary ranks is in conformity with the developmental situation of the Scheduled Tribes.

It may also be appropriate to call attention to some of the special features of the developmental situation in the states. In Bihar, the ranks on the industrial development of the Scheduled Tribes are better than those on the industrial growth of the non-Scheduled Tribes by extremely wide margins in all the years and the margins have increased progressively. This situation cannot be satisfactorily explained by the *medium-medium* ranks on the structural variables which, though consistent, do not form the ideal combination consistent with the wide margins. A supplementary explanation would lie in the fact that more than in any other state, the Scheduled Tribes in Bihar have been subjected to considerable developmental activities by the Christian missionaries and others.

In Kerala, the relatively low rank on the population percentage of the Scheduled Tribes warrants a better rank on the industrial development of the Scheduled Tribes in relation to the industrial growth of the non-Scheduled Tribes. But the real situation is quite the contrary. The inequitable development of the Scheduled Tribes is, to some extent, in agreement with the relatively low rank on the population percentage of the Scheduled Castes. But, in this state, the Scheduled Castes too are suffering from inequitable development. Kerala is relatively backward in its economy and yet has maintained the highest degree of modernization, especially in education and non-agricultural occupations. Such a situation does engender an acute degree of competition in which the disadvantaged sections (such as the Scheduled Tribes and Castes) stand to lose the most. This may explain why neither the Scheduled Tribes nor the Scheduled Castes have been able to take advantage of the structural situation in their development.

As already pointed out, the developmental situation of the Scheduled Tribes in Orissa is not in agreement with the structural factors. At every point of time, the rank on the IEI is higher than that on the population percentage of the non-Scheduled Tribes, which is inconsistent with the state's highest rank on the percentage of the Scheduled Tribe population. It is possible that the disadvantage of the structural factor for the development of the Scheduled Tribes has been neutralized by the relatively high rate of economic growth in Orissa, which was among the more under-developed states to start with.

West Bengal's structural situation—with a medium rank on the percentage of Scheduled Tribe population and a high rank on the percentage of Scheduled Caste population—is favourable for an equitable rank on the development of the Scheduled Tribes. In fact, the rank on the IEI in 1971 met this expectation. But in 1961 and 1981 the IEI ranks were lower than expected. This may be attributed to the relative stagnancy in the economy of West Bengal.

Thus, a detailed examination of the industrial development of the Scheduled Tribes in each of the states shows that in most of the states (except Bihar, Kerala, Orissa and West Bengal to some extent), the difference between the ranks on the industrial devel-opment of the Scheduled Tribes and that on the industrial growth of the non-Scheduled Tribes can be satisfactorily explained by the pattern of the ranks on the structural factors—namely, the popula-tion percentage of the Scheduled Tribes and Castes. In exceptional cases, the intervention of some other significant factors has been noticed.

Growth and Development: Inter-District Patterns

Let us now see how far the patterns of growth and development of the Scheduled Tribes in the variables of modernization which are evident in inter-state comparisons are also discernible at an inter-district level in the various states. This exercise is confined to only those states in which the Scheduled Tribes are found in appreciable numbers and limited to the 1981 Census data.

Educational Growth and Development

In the country as a whole there is a high degree of correlation between the educational growth (percentage of literacy) of the Scheduled Tribes and the educational growth of the non-Scheduled

Tribes. But these correlations in the states where the districts are taken as units become much reduced (Table 6.14, column 1); in most of the states they are small and in Maharashtra it is practically non-existent. Only in Gujarat and Madhya Pradesh do they assume moderate proportions. The only plausible explanation is that these correlations become stronger as the Scheduled Tribes advance in their growth, as has been the case with the Scheduled Castes also.

The educational growth of the Scheduled Tribes bears a small to moderate degree of negative correlation with the population of the Scheduled Tribes in most states; where the correlations are positive they are negligible. This pattern agrees with the all-India findings (Table 6.14, column 2). There is also a small degree of correlation between the educational growth of the Scheduled Tribes and the population percentage of the Scheduled Castes in most states, but they take either positive or negative values in different states (Table 6.14, column 3) which is understandable.

On the whole, therefore, the educational growth of the Scheduled Tribes cannot be understood either in terms of the educational growth of the districts or structural factors. It departs from the corresponding pattern of the Scheduled Castes insofar as it is barely correlated with the educational growth of the district.

The pattern of educational development among the Scheduled Tribes, however, is a little more determinate. As one would expect, there are high to very high degree of correlations between the IEE scores of the Scheduled Tribes and the percentage of their literacy (Table 6.14, column 4). Also, as expected, the correlations between the IEE scores of Scheduled Tribes and the percentage of literacy among the non-Scheduled Tribes is either negligible or small (Table 6.14, column 5). So the educational growth of a region does not affect the educational development of the Scheduled Tribes.

The population percentages of the Scheduled Tribes and Scheduled Castes (Table 6.14, columns 6 and 7) bear varying degrees of correlations with the IEE scores of the Scheduled Tribes. In the case of the population percentage of the Scheduled Tribes, the correlations are mostly negative; in two states where they are positive, they are negligible in proportion. On the other hand, in the case of the population percentage of the Scheduled Castes where the coefficients are of substantial dimensions (as in Maharashtra and Rajasthan), they take positive values.

Table 6.14
Coefficients of Correlation of the Growth and Developmental Variables of the Scheduled Tribes in Education with their Significant Correlates in the Various States (1981)

State	Percentage of Literacy among STs Correlated with the Percentage of			Scores on IEE of STs Correlated with the Percentage of			
	Literacy among Non-STs	Population of STs	Population of SCs	Literacy among STs	Literacy among Non-STs	Population of STs	Population of SCs
	(1)	(2)	(3)	(4)	(5)	(6)	(7)
Andhra Pradesh	0.305	-0.634	-0.278	0.821	-0.156	-0.581	-0.325
Bihar	0.241	-0.526	0.020	0.900	-0.180	-0.671	0.104
Gujarat	0.571	-0.292	-0.241	0.902	0.296	-0.356	-0.313
Madhya Pradesh	0.519	0.178	-0.257	0.926	0.200	0.136	-0.183
Maharashtra	0.045	-0.254	0.388	0.890	0.316	-0.354	0.591
Orissa	0.214	0.159	-0.236	0.755	-0.330	-0.242	0.137
Rajasthan	0.381	-0.438	0.430	0.879	-0.008	-0.571	0.564
West Bengal	0.393	0.100	-0.104	0.798	-0.207	0.193	-0.121
India (includes 12 states)	0.734	-0.385	-0.426	0.650	-0.007	-0.468	-0.133

Source: *Census of India*, 1981, Primary Census Abstract, for General Population, for Scheduled Castes, and for Scheduled Tribes.

The sum and substance of the analysis of the growth and development of the Scheduled Tribes in education at the state level,
with the district as the unit, is that the patterns, by and large,
conform to the logic of our explanation, but they provide only
weak evidence in support of the explanation.

Urban Growth and Development

Regarding the urban growth and development of the Scheduled
Tribes, the evidence from our analysis at the state levels seems to
support our explanation quite convincingly. The urbanization of
the Scheduled Tribes is correlated with the urbanization of the
non-Scheduled Tribes in moderate to high degrees in most states,
and the pattern is in consonance with the all-India findings (Table
6.15, column 1). The structural factors show varying degrees of
correlation in different states. Predictably, where the population
percentage of the Scheduled Tribes has a small or higher degree of
correlation with their urbanization (Table 6.15, column 2), the
correlation is negative, and the correlation of the population percentage of the Scheduled Castes with the urbanization of the
Scheduled Tribes (Table 6.15, column 3) is positive when it is
substantial. In both respects, the correlations displayed by the
states are more in keeping with our explanation than those found
at the all-India level.

The pattern of urban development of the Scheduled Tribes is
very much in keeping with the trends in development of the
disadvantaged section revealed in this study. The urban development of the Scheduled Tribes in the various states is highly and
very highly correlated with their urban growth (Table 6.14,
column 4) in all the states except Maharashtra where this
correlation is of a moderate degree; this pattern is in agreement
with the degree of correlation at the all-India level.

The correlations of the IEU scores of the Scheduled Tribes with
the percentage of the urban population of non-Scheduled Tribes
are either small or negligible and mostly negative in value (Table
6.14, column 5). Thus, the growth in the urbanization of the
districts, rather than helping the Scheduled Tribes to develop, has
in some cases widened the gulf between them and the rest of the
population.

The high to very high degree of negative correlations in most of

Table 6.15

Coefficients of Correlation of the Growth and Developmental Variables of the Scheduled Tribes in Urbanization with their Significant Correlates in the Various States (1981)

State	Percentage of Urban Population among STs Correlated with the Percentage of			Scores on IEU of STs Correlated with the Percentage of			
	Urban Population among Non-STs	Population of STs	Population of SCs	Urban Population among STs	Urban Population among Non-STs	Population of STs	Population of SCs
	(1)	(2)	(3)	(4)	(5)	(6)	(7)
Andhra Pradesh	0.946	-0.581	-0.325	0.976	0.229	-0.710	0.070
Bihar	0.340	-0.671	0.104	0.842	-0.281	-0.805	0.324
Gujarat	0.279	-0.356	-0.313	0.892	-0.135	-0.674	0.358
Madhya Pradesh	0.518	0.136	-0.183	0.813	0.014	-0.594	0.299
Maharashtra	0.503	-0.354	0.591	0.577	-0.243	-0.193	0.422
Orissa	0.486	-0.242	0.137	0.692	-0.198	-0.626	0.242
Rajasthan	0.426	-0.571	0.564	0.858	-0.014	-0.834	0.138
West Bengal	0.789	0.193	-0.121	0.843	0.432	-0.675	-0.036
India (includes 12 states)	0.524	-0.133	-0.077	0.734	-0.119	-0.007	-0.021

Source: *Census of India*, 1981, Primary Census Abstract, for General Population. for Scheduled Castes, and for Scheduled Tribes.

the states between the IEU scores of the Scheduled Tribes and their population percentage makes it quite obvious that the size of their population is the greatest hurdle in their urban development (Table 6.14, column 6). Maharashtra again stands out as a notable exception. Maharashtra apart, for some inexplicable reason, the pattern of these correlations in the states is sharply at variance with the lack of any correlation found at the all-India level. But it is what is revealed in the states which is in agreement with the general pattern, including the observation in the case of the Scheduled Castes.

The coefficients of correlation between the IEU scores of the Scheduled Tribes and the population percentage of the Scheduled Castes are either small or negligible but mostly positive in value. In other words, the Scheduled Tribes derive only a marginal advantage in urban development from the over-representation of the Scheduled Caste population in their districts. It may be recalled that the Scheduled Castes under similar circumstances (over-representation of the population of Scheduled Tribes) stand to benefit relatively more in their urban development. The differential advantage to the two sections stemming from the over-representation of the opposite section agrees with the fact that the Scheduled Castes on the whole are better developed.

Industrial Growth and Development

When the situation of the Scheduled Tribes is compared with that of the Scheduled Castes, it is generally found that the correlations between the growth of any one section with that of the rest of the population in any variable are of lower degrees in the former case. This is particularly true of the correlations between the percentages of non-agricultural workers among the Scheduled Tribes and of those among the non-Scheduled Tribes (Table 6.16, column 1). Except in West Bengal where the correlation is very high, in all the other states they are small or negligible. The correlations in the states, however, do not reflect the correlation at the all-India level, which is of a high degree.

Whereas the correlations of the industrial growth of the Scheduled Tribes with that of the non-Scheduled Tribes are small, those with the population percentage of the Scheduled Tribes are, on the whole, high and negative in four out of the eight states as well as at

Table 6.16

Coefficients of Correlation of the Growth and Developmental Variables of the Scheduled Tribes in Industrialization with their Significant Correlates in the Various States (1981)

State	Percentage of Non-Agricultural Workers among STs Correlated with the Percentage of			Scores on IEI of STs Correlated with the Percentage of			
	Non-Agricultural Workers among Non-SC/STs	Population of STs	Population of SCs	Non-Agricultural Workers among STs	Non-Agricultural Workers among Non-SC/STs	Population of STs	Population of SCs
	(1)	(2)	(3)	(4)	(5)	(6)	(7)
Andhra Pradesh	−0.026	−0.789	−0.011	0.767	−0.544	−0.633	−0.063
Bihar	0.209	−0.690	0.382	0.889	−0.184	−0.887	0.434
Gujarat	0.168	−0.779	0.218	0.906	−0.226	−0.895	0.356
Madhya Pradesh	0.252	0.109	0.640	0.857	−0.169	−0.758	0.614
Maharashtra	0.245	−0.369	0.418	0.766	−0.255	−0.442	0.421
Orissa	0.423	−0.291	−0.099	0.830	0.066	−0.643	0.170
Rajasthan	0.377	−0.663	0.211	0.806	−0.140	−0.800	0.879
West Bengal	0.725	−0.079	0.218	0.911	0.457	−0.011	0.302
India (includes 12 states)	0.671	−0.776	0.100	0.803	−0.017	−0.670	0.521

Source: *Census of India*, 1981, Primary Census Abstract, for General Population, for Scheduled Castes, and for Scheduled Tribes.

the all-India level (Table 6.16, column 2). Thus the correlation of the percentage of their own population with their growth variable is more marked in the case of the industrial growth of the Scheduled Tribes than in their educational and urban growth. The correlations of industrial growth with the population percentage of the Scheduled Castes in most of the states are small and of positive value, which are as expected (Table 6.16, column 3). Only in Madhya Pradesh is this correlation uncommonly high (0.640).

The correlations of the IEI scores (industrial development) with each of the variables of the percentage of non-agricultural workers among the Scheduled Tribes, the percentage of non-agricultural workers among the non-Scheduled Tribes, the percentage of the population of the Scheduled Tribes, and the percentage of the population of the Scheduled Castes (Table 6.16, columns 4, 5, 6 and 7) in most states follow the expected patterns and that too in accentuated forms. Industrial development is highly or very highly correlated with the industrial growth of the Scheduled Tribes themselves, but shows little or no relationship with the growth of the non-Scheduled Tribes/Castes.

Except in West Bengal, the correlations of industrial development of the Scheduled Tribes with the percentage of the population of the Scheduled Tribes shows moderate to very high degrees and the values in all cases are negative (Table 6.16, column 6). On the other hand, the correlations between industrial development and the population of the Scheduled Castes are mostly small and positive; they are negligible in two states and high in two others (Table 6.16, column 7).

Taking all the three developmental variables, it may be concluded that in none of them does the growth of the district as a whole play a facilitating role; on the contrary, in most cases the growth of the non-Scheduled Tribes has even retarded the development of the Scheduled Tribes. The size of their own population has come in the way of the development of the Scheduled Tribes in most cases and the constraining role of the population size is very pronounced in urban and industrial development. On the other hand, the size of the population of the Scheduled Castes has played a facilitating role but, in most cases, in a small way. With a few exceptions, the pattern of correlations in the states corresponds with the relevant correlations at the all-India level. So also the developmental patterns of the Scheduled Tribes, on the whole, follow those of the Scheduled Castes.

The findings of our analysis at the state level (with districts as the units) fit our explanatory scheme even better than the analysis at the all-India level (with states as the units).

Comparison of the Development Patterns in the Three Variables

In order to obtain a total picture of the correlations of all the three developmental variables (IEE, IEU and IEI) with the variables of special significance to us, the relevant correlations, converted into scores, are presented in Table 6.17. It is worth commenting upon some of the broad features which can be easily discerned from the table even though, sometimes, it may be a repetition of earlier observations.

In all columns except one, the pattern of the correlation scores of the states is consistent with the score for the country. The exception is the column which refers to the correlation between the IEU and the population percentage of the Scheduled Tribes. In this case, the score for the country in 1981 shown in this table is totally at variance with the corresponding correlation in 1971 (see Table 6.10), which is closer to the scores of the states in Table 6.17, column 5. Moreover, the scores of the states are in accord with our explanation.

Although the scores at the all-India level are mostly consistent with those at the state level, they also cover up the differences between states.

It is true of all the developmental variables that their correlations with their corresponding variables pertaining to the growth of the non-Scheduled Tribes (Table 6.17, columns 1, 4 and 7), in the various states, are closer to the negligible value and are more on the negative side especially in the case of industrialization (column 7). It shows that development planning, rather than bridging the gap between the Scheduled Tribes and the non-Scheduled Tribes in their modernization, has often increased it.

The structural variable of the population of the Scheduled Tribes is negatively correlated with their development in every variable (Table 6.17, columns 2, 5 and 7); however, the correlations become stronger when we move from column 2 to 5 and from column 5 to 8. The correlations of the population percentage of the Scheduled Castes with the development of the Scheduled Castes can be seen in most of the states in all the variables, but

Table 6.17

Scores on the Coefficients of Correlation of Each of the Developmental Variables of Education, Urbanization and Industrialization of the Scheduled Tribes with the Corresponding Growth Variables of the Non-Scheduled Tribes and with the Population Percentage of the Scheduled Tribes and Castes in the Various States (1981)

State	IEE Scores Correlated with the Percentage of			IEU Scores Correlated with the Percentage of			IEI Scores Correlated with the Percentage of		
	Literate Non-STs (1)	ST Population (2)	SC Population (3)	Urban Non-STs (4)	ST Population (5)	SC Population (6)	Industrial Non-STs (7)	ST Population (8)	SC Population (9)
Andhra Pradesh	–0	–2	–1	1	–3	0	–2	–3	–0
Bihar	–0	–3	0	–1	–4	1	–0	–4	2
Gujarat	1	–1	–1	–0	–3	1	–1	–4	1
Madhya Pradesh	1	0	–0	0	–2	1	–0	–3	3
Maharashtra	1	–1	2	–1	–0	2	–1	–2	2
Orissa	–1	–1	0	–0	–3	1	0	–3	0
Rajasthan	–0	–2	2	–0	–4	1	–0	–4	4
West Bengal	–1	0	–0	2	–3	–0	2	–0	1
India	–0	–2	–0	–0	–0	–0	–0	–3	2

Source: Table 6.13 for Cols. 1–3; Table 6.15 for Cols. 4–6; and Table 6.16 for Cols. 7–9.

Note: As the score 0 takes + or – values from 0 to 0.19 degrees, some of the 0 scores in the table assume negative signs.

Degrees of Correlation	Scores
0–0.19	0
0.2–0.39	1
0.4–0.59	2
0.6–0.79	3
0.8+	4

they are decidedly positive only in the cases of the IEU and IEI, and quite strong only in the case of the IEI. The scores on the correlation between the developmental variables and the population percentage are consistently high in Bihar where the Scheduled Tribes have shown the highest levels of development, relatively speaking; on the other hand, they are low on the whole in West Bengal, where the relative development of the Scheduled Tribes is much lower. This indicates that as development accelerates, the structural constraint represented by their population becomes stronger.

Comparison of the Development Patterns among the Scheduled Tribes and Castes and non-Scheduled Tribes and Castes

It is clear from our earlier analysis (see Chapters 4, 5 and 6) that the Scheduled Tribes and Castes and non-Scheduled Tribes and Castes in any state have unequal opportunities of development. A comparison of the ranks of the Scheduled Tribes and Castes and the non-Scheduled Tribes and Castes on the values of their developmental variables of education, urbanization and industrialization may be instructive. The relevant information is given in Table 6.18. It may be pointed out that in the case of the non-Scheduled Tribes and Castes, their percentage distribution in the respective variables has been treated as the indexes of their development. Being the dominant section, it is assumed that their growth is unaffected by the growth of the disadvantaged sections and hence, in their case, growth itself represents development. Further, only the eight states in which the Scheduled Tribes are adequately represented are considered for this comparison.

It should, however, be borne in mind that this comparison is not aimed at seeing which section is more advanced, a conclusion which has been reached already; in every state, the non-Scheduled Tribes and Castes are the most advanced, the Scheduled Tribes are the least advanced and the Scheduled Castes fall in between. This comparison is based on the assumption of the principle of integration at two levels. It is assumed that under conditions of perfect integration, first there will be a perfect correlation among the three variables of development in each of the population categories; that is, the ranks of a state under all the three columns of any of the sets—1, 2, 3; 4, 5, 6; and 7, 8, 9 in Table 6.18—would be the same. Second, there would be a correlation among the ranks of the three population groups in the various states so that the ranks of a state under all the nine columns will be the same. The argument here is that the extent to which the ranks deviate from the ideal-typical pattern would depend upon the various factors discussed in this study.

An examination of the ranks of the developmental variables within each of the population categories in Table 6.18 shows that the three ranks of a state in a population category are very rarely identical, there being only three such instances—those of the Scheduled Tribes in Bihar, the Scheduled Castes in Gujarat and the non-Scheduled Tribes and Castes also in Gujarat. The co-efficients of correlation between the different pairs of variables in the three population categories (Table 6.19) show that there is a relatively high degree of integration among the Scheduled Castes and the non-Scheduled Tribes/Castes, but among the Scheduled Tribes it is low to moderate in two pairs of variables and absent in the third pair between education and industrialization. Even among the other two population categories, the correlation between education and industrialization is the lowest.

The lack of correlation between the developmental variables of education and industrialization found among the Scheduled Tribes would indicate that most of the non-agricultural occupations followed by these people are at low levels of prestige, which do not require education. Therefore, the relatively high ranks on the industrialization of the Scheduled Tribes, especially in Andhra Pradesh and West Bengal (Table 6.18, column 3), may not imply higher levels of development.

Although the ranks of the three variables of a population category in a state are not identical in most cases, when we compare a cluster of three variables in a population category with the clusters in the other two categories, it forms a distinct entity (Table 6.17). Therefore, when we make broad comparisons among the developmental patterns of the Scheduled Tribes and Castes, and the non-Scheduled Tribes and Castes, we find some striking differences in the situations of the different categories. In Bihar, the developmental situation of the Scheduled Tribes is far superior to that of the Scheduled Castes or the non-Scheduled Tribes and Castes, whereas in Gujarat and Madhya Pradesh the situation of

Table 6.18

Comparison of the Scheduled Tribes and Castes and Non-Scheduled Tribes and Castes According to their Ranks on the Developmental Variables in the Various States (1981)

State	Developmental Variables among STs			Developmental Variables among SCs			Percentages of Non-SC/ST Population in		
	IEE	IEU	IEI	IEE	IEU	IEI	Literacy	Urbanization	Non-Agricultural Workers
	(1)	(2)	(3)	(4)	(5)	(6)	(7)	(8)	(9)
Andhra Pradesh	8	4	3	5	7	8	6	5	4
Bihar	1	1	1	8	6	6	7	8	8
Gujarat	3	5	7	1	1	1	2	2	2
Madhya Pradesh	6	7	8	3	3	2	5	4	5
Maharashtra	2	3	5	2	2	3	1	1	3
Orissa	5	2	4	4	5	5	4	7	7
Rajasthan	4	6	6	6	4	4	8	6	6
West Bengal	7	8	2	6	8	7	3	3	1

Source: Tables 6.3, 6.6 and 6.9 for Cols. 1, 2, and 3 respectively; Table 4.18 for Cols. 4, 5 and 6; while Cols. 7, 8 and 9 have been derived from *Census of India*, 1981; Primary Census Abstract, for General Population, for Scheduled Castes, and for Scheduled Tribes.

Table 6.19

Correlations among the Developmental Variables in Eight States in the Different Population Categories

Population Categories	Pairs of Variables Correlated		
	Education & Urbanization	Education & Industrialization	Urbanization & Industrialization
STs	0.571	0	0.404
SCs	0.789	0.739	0.952
Non-ST/SCs	0.810	0.690	0.881

the Scheduled Castes is decidedly favourable in comparison with the other two categories. In Orissa, both the Scheduled Tribes and the Scheduled Castes enjoy, on the whole, higher developmental ranks as compared with the non-Scheduled Tribes and Castes. West Bengal presents yet another striking situation; here (if we ignore the high rank of the Scheduled Tribes on industrialization), both the Scheduled Tribes and the Scheduled Castes occupy extremely disadvantageous ranks compared with the ranks of the non-Scheduled Tribes and Castes. In Maharashtra also, the ranks of the Scheduled Tribes and the Scheduled Castes are lower than those of the non-Scheduled Tribes and Castes but the differences are small.

The earlier discussions would explain why the developmental situations of the different population categories are what they are in the different states. I shall only add that the analysis of the developmental situations of the different population categories would broaden our understanding of the different configurations of the social, economic and political relations in different states. Moreover, it will provide insights for the reformulation of the strategies of planning.

7

Summary and Implications

Summary

Although moralistic in its conception, since it is aimed at bringing about a desired kind of person and society, the idea of development may be viewed from two broad perspectives. Whereas, according to one perspective, the growth of the economy through industrialism gives rise to the desired type of person, according to the other, the economic and social structure should be **manipulated** so as to enable the desired type of person to emerge. Depending on the perspective adopted, development planning can be regarded either as economy-centred or as individual-centred. For present purposes, planning aimed at developing the economy may be considered to be growth-oriented while that which is directly aimed at shaping the desired kind of society and person to be development-oriented, because it is the latter type of planning which has to grapple with the moral issues implied in the concept of development.

It would appear that economic planners, although they may not state it explicitly, subscribe to the idea of economic reductionism whereby it is assumed that economic growth suitably modifies the social structure, leading to social progress. In doing so, however, they reckon without the reality of the autonomy and resilience of the social structure. The social structure essentially consists of groupings based on primordial ties and shaped by history. In a sense, the social structure represents the indelible marks of history, which are not easy to be erased, such as the case of Indian society which reflects the history of over five thousand years.

Because of the thousands of years of dominant-subordinate relationships between groupings, any society has a cumulation of structural injustices which are sought to be removed or at least reduced by development planning. The structural injustices are, no doubt, affected by economic changes and are capable of being minimized through economic planning. But mere economic change or growth is not sufficient for the reduction of structural injustices; to achieve such an objective, economic change has to be specially tailored to suit the objective. If economic change is not directly aimed at changing the social structure in the desired direction, the latter has the capacity to channel the former according to its own design.

Whereas it is true that development planning in India is inspired by the moral principles of the Constitution and that the basic objectives of planning are also set on a moral plane in the Plan documents, in its actual implementation, it is expediency rather than moral and social values which has guided Indian planning. Consequently, whereas planning has certainly brought about changes in society, the society has not taken the desired course. This study is aimed at showing the response of the social structure to development planning.

The Indian social structure, with its peculiar caste, ethnic, religious and tribal formations, is characterized by deep-seated structural injustices which pose formidable obstacles to the development of individuals. Since development planning has not been directly aimed at removing structural injustices, it has not succeeded in reducing the inequitous character of the social structure. On the contrary, the fruits of development have gone to the people according to their position in the social structure, those occupying higher positions benefiting much more than those occupying the lower ones.

Because of the long-abiding caste character of the Indian society, even at the higher rungs, different castes have different economic interests. Consequently, in a given region, the rural and urban economies are controlled by different castes. So, also, the elite groups of different religious categories living in a region usually belong to different castes with conflicting economic interests. Poverty in India is mainly a structural attribute; it is the same castes and tribes, which are socio-culturally marginal, which have continued to be poor for centuries. The planned process of modernization channelled through such an inequitous social structure accentuates the structural injustices and sharpens the clash of interests.

Of particular significance is the clash of interests between the rural and urban elites. Whereas both these categories have benefited from planned economic development, in industrial-oriented economic growth the urban elites stand to gain to a much larger extent. Added to this is the predicament encountered by the rural elites who, when experiencing a phenomenal population growth in the face of limited opportunities in the rural economy, are compelled to seek opportunities in the growing urban economy which is controlled by members of other groups. The problem is further confounded by the fact that the urban economies of some regions are controlled by migrant groups from other regions. This is only an illustration to show that when economic change is channelled through the existing social structure, it nevertheless disturbs the old balance of relations between social groupings. This study has only touched upon problems such as these.

The major thrust of this study, however, is a detailed examination of the way in which the Scheduled Castes and Scheduled Tribes—the two most underprivileged segments of Indian society—have reacted to the modernizing process of planning. The analysis, which is based on the available information from the Census publications, is rather coarse as the data used stand for only the indicators of the variables examined. The percentages of literacy, urbanization and non-agricultural workers in the population are taken to be the indexes of modernization. An increase in these percentages would indicate a growth in modernization. For a comparative picture, the data at three points of time—1961, 1971 and 1981—are examined.

The measurement of variables used in this analysis hardly does justice to the concept of development elaborated in the study. Since the measure had to be tailored to the available data, the idea of development is captured by the notion of equity. This is done by measuring the growth of the underprivileged section, in a given variable of modernization, in relation to the growth of the rest of the population in that variable; the index value is obtained by multiplying this value by 100. The analysis has focused on seeing to what extent the growth and development of the Scheduled Castes and Tribes follow the pattern of development planning, and on identifying the causes of the variations, if any, from the expected pattern.

For the most part, in the analysis the Scheduled Castes or the Scheduled Tribes are treated as an omnibus category. The caste

differences among the Scheduled Castes and the tribal differentiation among the Scheduled Tribes have been ignored. The units
used for analysis are geographical/administrative areas, such as the
larger states in the country and the districts in the states. However,
caste or tribal differences in growth and development are equally
important. An idea about the significance of such differences for
growth and development has been given in the analysis of the
educational growth and development of the Scheduled Castes in
the state of Punjab.

The analysis is done at two levels: first, on a larger scale, the
country as a whole is treated as the universe and the larger states
as the units. Second, on a smaller scale, each of the larger states
has been taken to be the universe and the districts as units. The
effectiveness of planning on the modernization of the disadvantaged
sections is gauged from the degree of correlation between the
growth and development of these sections, on the one hand, and
the growth in the modernization of the rest of the population. The
structural factors are represented by the population percentages of
the Scheduled Castes and Tribes in the total population.

The findings show that both the Scheduled Castes and Tribes
fall far behind the rest of the population in their levels of modernization. But, between the two categories, the Scheduled Castes on
the whole, are more modernized than the Scheduled Tribes. Such
a situation agrees with the fact that whereas both the Scheduled
Castes and Tribes are marginal to the mainstream society, the
former are relatively more integrated with it. The effect of planning
percolates down to the Scheduled Castes faster than it does to the
Scheduled Tribes. The modernization levels of both the categories
have risen from 1961 to 1981 both in the absolute and relative (in
comparison with the rest of the society) sense.

By and large, the patterns of modernization are similar among
both the Scheduled Castes and Tribes. There are, no doubt, some
differences, but they stem primarily from the fact that the Scheduled Tribes are at a lower level of modernization. What is still
more significant is the fact that the patterns of modernization
revealed in the larger scale of analysis (with the country as the
universe) are also, by and large, replicated at a lower scale of
analysis (with the states as the universe). The differences in some
cases can be attributed to special circumstances. So also, with
minor exceptions, the patterns of modernization in the three

different variables of education, urbanization and industrialization are similar. Thus, the modernization of the Scheduled Castes and the Scheduled Tribes is systematic.

It is useful to note that the distinction that is made between growth (level of modernization) and development (growth in relation to the level of modernization of the rest of the society) of the underprivileged throws light on two kinds of problems faced by these sections in their modernization. An examination of the growth shows that in the process of modernization the inequalities among the Scheduled Castes or the Scheduled Tribes belonging to the different castes or tribes and belonging to different geographical/administrative areas are widening very rapidly. On the other hand, the indexes of development show the inequalities of the underprivileged vis-a-vis the modernization of the rest of the society. There is also a wide degree of variation in the development. However, it is interesting to note that the correlates of growth and development in modernization are quite different. It shows that somewhat different sets of strategies are needed in order to solve these varied types of problems.

The growth of the Scheduled Castes or the Scheduled Tribes is highly correlated with the level of modernization of the rest of the society in the area they live. In other words, planning directly affects the modernization of the underprivileged through the trickle-down effect. But the trickle-down effect varies according to the level of modernization of the area they inhabit—the higher the level, the greater is the trickle-down effect. This is the reason why the inequalities between the underprivileged in the different states or districts are widening. Usually the underprivileged living in the most modernized administrative area are also the most modernized, whereas those living in the least modernized area are, likewise, the least modernized. In general, it is also found that the rate of advancement of the most modernized state is also the highest, and that of the least modernized one is the least. This explains why the relative positions in modernization of the underprivileged in the different states remain more or less constant and the inequalities between those who are the most modernized and the least modernized are widening.

There is also a similar situation of the widening of inequalities among the castes of the Scheduled Castes and the tribes of the Scheduled Tribes. There are two major reasons for the widening of the inequalities among the different Scheduled Castes, as illustrated by the educational growth of the Scheduled Castes in the state of Punjab. First, the different Scheduled Castes living in a given geographical area form a hierarchy on the indexes of modernization, and the castes which are at a higher level advance faster than those at lower levels. Second, the different castes are spread in different geographical areas; those residing in the more developed areas advance faster than those living in the backward areas. As a result of these two trends, the caste at the apex of the Scheduled Caste hierarchy in the geographical area which is most advanced will advance most rapidly and the caste which is at the bottom of the Scheduled Caste hierarchy in the geographical area which is least developed will grow most tardily. Thus, the gulf between the most advanced and the least advanced castes keeps on widening.

When we come to the development of the underprivileged, however, the respective variables (with the exception of education to some extent) show either a negligible or negative correlation with the modernization of the rest of the population. It shows that whereas the trickle-down effect due to the global planning strategy has an impact on the bottom layers in direct proportion to the level of modernization of the higher strata, it does not ensure that the bottom layers have the same opportunities as the upper layers. In fact, in the initial stages of modernization, the differences between the higher and the lower strata actually increase, thus giving rise to a negative correlation between the development of the underprivileged and the modernization of the rest of the population in some cases. The negative relationship is more often noticeable in the case of the Scheduled Tribes who are relatively less exposed to planning than the Scheduled Castes.

However, the correlation between the development of the underprivileged and the modernization of the rest of the population reaches a significant degree in the case of education, but only among the Scheduled Castes. It is only in the case of education that the Scheduled Castes and Tribes are also given target-group treatment. This has probably enabled the Scheduled Castes, who are relatively more modernized, to take greater advantage of the educational opportunities in the more modernized states or districts.

In general, whereas planning has not influenced the development of the underprivileged commensurate with the level of modernization of the rest of the population, there is strong evidence to show that their development is influenced by structural factors which are represented by their population percentages. In the case of the Scheduled Castes, their development is negatively correlated with the percentage of their own population but positively correlated with the percentage of the population of the Scheduled Tribes. *Mutatis mutandis*, the same pattern holds good in the case of the Scheduled Tribes. In general terms, when the two categories of underprivileged live together, the development of any one category is negatively correlated with the population of that category but positively correlated with the population of the other category. The positive correlation with population of the other category is relatively higher in the case of the Scheduled Castes, which agrees with the fact that the Scheduled Castes, as compared with the Scheduled Tribes, are better modernized.

The influence of structural factors is rather subdued in the case of the development in industrialization (non-agricultural occupations). This does not mean that in this case there is a greater degree of influence of planning. It is possible that the variable of non-agricultural occupations does not represent the essence of modernization to the same extent as education and urbanization do.

The structural factors also affect the growth in modernization, but to a much lesser degree, so that the effect of planning stands out.

Thus it is clear that, by and large, the higher levels of development achieved by the underprivileged in some of the states or districts are not due so much to the progressive measures of planning but to the fortuitous circumstances created by the structural factors. It is obvious that in states such as Gujarat and Madhya Pradesh, the relatively higher levels of development of the Scheduled Castes, and in states such as Punjab and Uttar Pradesh, their relatively lower levels, are mainly due to the relatively lower percentage of Scheduled Caste population and the higher percentage of Scheduled Tribe population in the first set of states and due to the reverse trends in these variables in the second set.

Because of the opposite effect of the population percentage of their own group in relation to the other group on their development, when both the Scheduled Castes and Tribes are living in a state or district they tend to have, relatively speaking, unequal levels of development; in some states the Scheduled Castes are doing relatively better and in some others the Scheduled Tribes. In rare cases, however, they are on par with each other, but this may be treated as an exception. The exceptional cases can be used to understand the role of special circumstances in the development of the underprivileged (as in the states of West Bengal, Tamil Nadu and Orissa).

In West Bengal, both the Scheduled Castes and Tribes fare equally badly in their development as compared with the general pattern, even after allowing for the effect of structural factors. A factor which can be linked with this peculiar situation is the relatively slow rate of economic growth of West Bengal, as a result of which the state has been coming down in its position among the states in the country on its level of economic development. It appears that it is mainly the underprivileged who have lost out in this decline, while the higher strata, by and large, have been able to hold their own. The unduly low level of development of the Scheduled Castes in Tamil Nadu also may be attributed, to some extent, to the relatively poor economic showing of this state. Contrariwise, the relatively better developmental standing of both the Scheduled Castes and Tribes in Orissa may be linked with the relatively rapid strides taken by this state in economic growth. It would appear from these examples that a quicker tempo of economic growth is more conducive to the better development of the underprivileged. When the economy backfires, the bottom-most strata get hit the hardest. Thus, even the forces generated by the vicissitudes of economic development also get transformed through the social structure.

This summary is being concluded on a note of caution. The measures of growth and advancement of the underprivileged and their overall improvement from 1961 to 1981 should not be taken to mean their exact levels of advancement in comparison with the rest of the population. Since we have considered their modernization in terms of very broad variables, it is possible that their relative advancement is exaggerated by the indicators used. For example, in education they are over-represented at the lower levels, in urbanization, in the slums and fringes of towns and cities, and in industrialization, in the inferior, informal sector of the economy. Therefore, an index score of 100 on development does not mean that they are on par with the rest of the population in modernization. Nevertheless, the measures are useful in delineating the trends of modernization.

Implications for Planning

During the four decades of its history, planning in India has had, perforce, to make several modifications in its approaches and strategy, which is an indication of its dynamism. Starting with a economic-sectoral approach, it soon had to incorporate the regional planning approach to cope with the growing regional disparities. Then, with the realization that the global strategy of planning did not uplift the weaker sections, this strategy was supplemented with target-group planning, particularly with the introduction of some rural development schemes. The Plans have also tried to incorporate the Constitutional provisions of protective discrimination for the underprivileged. Currently, a serious debate is going on about decentralizing the planning procedures by introducing what is termed 'grass-root' planning with a view to generate a greater degree of public participation in the planning process. All these are welcome developments in the evolution of the planning process in India. One may, therefore, well ask, what are the implications of this study for planning purposes?

Despite all the modifications, planning in India is overtly concerned with economic growth. The Plan targets are mostly set in terms of economic growth rates and rarely in terms of the indicators of distributive justice. This study calls attention to the more fundamental goals of planning which are concerned with ushering in a just society. It has been shown that so far as the social structure is concerned, whereas planning has generated many changes, it has not been able to channel them in the desired direction; society has gone beyond the control of the planning process.

Already, with economic development, the cleavages in society are becoming even more ominous. In the rural areas in any region, one or two caste groups have monopolized the ownership of land and, likewise, in the urban areas people from a handful of caste and ethnic groups control the commercial, industrial and administrative sectors. The vast majority of the population, both in the rural and urban areas, is without any assets worth mentioning. Unemployment, especially among the educated youth, is assuming alarming proportions. In the ever-growing urban sector, the population living in slums and which belongs mostly to the underprivileged sections, is growing much faster than that of the nonslum areas. To take a typical case: in Bombay, the slum population comprised only 12 per cent of the city's population in 1961. However, it grew to 22 per cent and 45 per cent in 1971 and 1981 respectively, and is currently estimated to be between 55 and 60 per cent. If this is the state of affairs in the commercial capital of the country during the period of planned development, one can imagine the environmental and housing situation in the other large cities in the country.

Gigantic soical problems (such as the ones just mentioned) cast serious doubt on the suitability of the current mode of planning and, in fact, on the suitability of the evolutionary mode of planning itself, to bring about the desired kind of change. At least they call for a drastic change in the method of setting the goals of planning; it is not the rate of growth of the economy per se, but the degree of fulfilment of human needs and the elimination of glaring inequalities in society which should be the yardstick of the success of planning. However, on a modest plane, in the instant case of the development of the Scheduled Castes and Tribes, we may draw on some implications of the findings of this study to improve the planning strategy.

This study has clearly distinguished between two broad types of problems with regard to the growth and development of the underprivileged in their modernization which can be linked with the planning strategies. One of the problems is that of growing inequalities among the sub-groupings within an underprivileged category itself; the other problem is that of the relative deprivation of the underprivileged category vis-a-vis the rest of the population. The causes of the two types of problems are also to a large extent different. But both types of problems are the by-products of the global strategy of planning. First, this strategy enables the better-off groupings as well as those living in more advanced geographical areas among the underprivileged to advance faster, which increases the inequalities within the underprivileged category. Second, it enables the priviledged sections to advance much faster than the underprivileged ones, thereby perpetuating the relative inequalities between the privileged and the underprivileged.

Therefore, if one of the objectives of planning is to provide equal opportunities of advancement for the underprivileged then, in order to make up for their centuries-old handicaps, they should be given favoured treatment through target-group planning. The efficacy of this technique is demonstrated to some extent by the better results achieved with regard to the educational development of the Scheduled Castes, where the underprivileged could also take advantage of favoured treatment. The present policy of target-group planning is, however, rather haphazard and not based on considered reasoning. Target-group planning can be made effective only when the development idea of 'putting the last first' is made the sheet-anchor of planning.

One of the major shortcomings of the limited amount of favoured treatment already being given to the underprivileged is that it is the category as a whole (such as the Scheduled Castes or the Scheduled Tribes) which has been taken as the target, disregarding the internal differentiation, which is responsible for the undesirable trend of growing inequalities within the category; the special handicaps of the relatively more deprived among the underprivileged are not given due consideration. On the other hand, the complexity of the problem of the relative deprivation of the underprivileged as a category is due to neglect of the structural factors.

Our delineation of the constraints on the modernizing trends among the underprivileged shows that the regional inequalities among them are inextricably linked with the regional imbalances in general and, therefore, the promotion of a more equitable trend of modernization depends partly upon the integration of the development of the underprivileged with the policy of an equitable development for the regions. If in regional planning, the more backward regions are given target-group treatment, it will have a relatively greater trickle-down (global) impact on the more deprived underprivileged living in those regions. In order to reduce the inequalities between the underprivileged and the rest of the population, target groups need to be formed on the basis of structural factors which vary from region to region and within each region according to caste/tribal distinctions. The demarcation of such groupings would enable the planners to identify the ones which deserve more favoured treatment.

There are, of course, a number of other issues, such as, for example, the types of programmes, which have to be considered in the formation of policies for the development of the underprivileged, which are beyond the scope of our analysis. This study, above all, should help specify the Plan objectives which are pivotal in policy-making for the underprivileged.

References

Ardrey, Robert. 1966. *The Territorial Imperative*, London, Collins.

Bailey, F.C. 1958. *Caste and the Economic Frontier*, Bombay, Oxford University Press.

Census of India, 1961, Volume I—India, Part II-A(i), General Population Tables.

Census of India, 1961, Volume I—India, Part V-A(i), Special Tables for Scheduled Castes.

Census of India, 1961, Volume I—India, Part V-A(ii), Special Tables for Scheduled Tribes.

Census of India, 1971, Series 1—India, Union Primary Census Abstract.

Census of India, 1971, Series 1—India, Part V-A(i), Special Tables for Scheduled Castes.

Census of India, 1971, Series 1—India, Part V-A(ii), Special Tables for Scheduled Tribes.

Census of India, 1981, Series 1—India, Part II B(i), Primary Census Abstract, General Population.

Census of India, 1981, Series 1—India, Part II B(ii), Primary Census Abstract, Scheduled Castes.

Census of India, 1981, Series 1—India, Part II B(iii), Primary Census Abstract, Scheduled Tribes.

Chakravarty, Sukhamoy. 1987. *Development Planning: The Indian Experience*, Oxford, Clarendon Press.

Chitnis, Suma. 1972. 'Education for Equality: Case of Scheduled Castes,' *Economic and Political Weekly*, Vol. VII, Nos 31–33, Special Number, pp. 1675–81.

Dandekar, V.M. 1988. 'Indian Economy Since Independence,' *Economic and Political Weekly*, Vol. XXIII, Nos 1 and 2, 2–9 January, pp. 41–50.

—————. 1987. 'Let the Workers Own and Manage,' Presidential Address, 28th Annual Conference of Indian Society of Labour Economics, Tiruchirapalli.

Dandekar, V.M. and N. Rath. 1971. *Poverty in India*, Pune, Indian School of Political Economy.

Dantwala, M.L. 1987. 'Equality: The Forgotten Ideal,' IASSI Quarterly Newsletter, Vol. 6, No. 2, pp. 14–18.

D'Souza, Victor S. 1980. *Educational Inequalities Among Scheduled Castes: A Case Study in the Punjab*, Department of Sociology, Panjab University.

—————. 1981. *Inequality and Its Perpetuation*, New Delhi, Manohar Publications.

—————. 1982. 'Economy, Caste, Religion and Population Distribution: An Analysis of Communal Tension in Punjab,' *Economic and Political Weekly*, Vol. XVII, No. 19, pp. 783–92.

—————. 1983. 'Religious Minorities in India: A Demographic Analysis,' *Social Action*, Vol. 33, October–December.

D'Souza, Victor S. 1985. *Economic Development, Social Structure and Population Growth*, New Delhi, Sage Publications.

Eisenstadt, S.N. 1964. 'Social Change, Differentiation and Evolution,' *The American Sociological Review*, Vol. 29, No. 3, pp. 373–86.

Firth, Raymond. 1964. *Essay on Social Organization and Values*, London, Athlone Press.

Friedmann, John. 1987. *Planning in the Public Domain: From Knowledge to Action*, Princeton, Princeton University Press.

Fromm, Erich. 1979. *To Have or To Be*, London, Sphere Books.

Galanter, Marc. 1984. *Competing Equalities: Law and the Backward Classes in India*, Delhi, Oxford University Press.

Galtung, Johan, Roy Preiswerk and **Monica Wimegah.** 1982. 'Development Centred on the Human Beings: Some West European Perspectives,' UNESCO, 1982, pp. 82–114.

Gill, Manmohan Singh. 1983. 'Socio-Ecological Development of Small Towns: A Comparative Study of a Manufacturing and Trade Town,' Thesis submitted to Panjab University, unpublished.

Government of India. 1985. *Statewise Information on Education of Scheduled Castes and Scheduled Tribes*, New Delhi, Ministry of Education.

Hodge, Robert W., Paul M. Siegel and **Peter H. Rossi,** 1964. 'Occupational Prestige in the United States, 1925–63,' *American Journal of Sociology*, Vol. 70, pp. 286–302.

Hodge, Robert W., Donald J. Treiman and **Peter H. Rossi.** 1965. 'A Comparative Study of Occupational Prestige,' presented at the Annual Meeting of the American Sociological Society, Chicago.

Hsu, Francis L.K. 1977. 'Individual Fulfilment, Social Stability and Cultural Progress,' in Gordon J. Direnzo, ed., *We the People, American Character and Social Changes*, Westport, Connecticut, Greenwood Press.

Inkeles, Alex. 1960. 'Industrial Man: The Relation of Status to Experience, Perception and Values,' *The American Journal of Sociology*, Vol. 66, pp. 1–31.

Inkeles, Alex and **David H. Smith.** 1974. *Becoming Modern: Individual Change in Six Developing Countries*, Cambridge, Mass., Harvard University Press.

Inkeles, Alex and **Peter H. Rossi.** 1956. 'National Comparisons of Occupational Prestige,' *The American Journal of Sociology*, Vol. 61, pp. 329–39.

Lagos, Gustavo. 1975. 'The Revolution of Being,' in Saul H. Mendlovitz, ed., *On the Creation of a Just World Order*, New Delhi, Orient Longman, pp. 71–110.

Loubser, Jan J. 1982. 'Development Centred on Man: Some Relevant Concepts from Canada,' Paris, UNESCO.

Moore, Wilbert E. 1960. 'A Reconsideration of Theories of Social Change,' *The American Sociological Review*, Vol. 25, No. 6, pp. 810–18.

Nathan, Dev. 1987. 'Structure of Working Class in India,' *Economic and Political Weekly*, Vol. XXII, No. 18, pp. 799–809.

Nautiyal, K.C. and **Y.D. Sharma.** 1978. *Equalization of Educational Opportunities for Scheduled Castes and Scheduled Tribes*, New Delhi, NCERT.

Parsons, Talcott. 1964. 'Evolutionary Universals in Society,' *The American Sociological Review*, Vol. 29, No. 3, pp. 339–57.

Planning Commission, Government of India, 1985. *Seventh Five-Year Plan 1985–90*, New Delhi, Controller of Publications.

Randall, Jr., John Herman. 1965. *The Career of Philosophy*, Vol. 2, New York. Columbia University Press.

Rostow, W.W. 1961. *The Stages of Economic Growth: A Non-Communist Manifesto*, Cambridge, Cambridge University Press.

Sachs, Ignacy. 1978. 'Crises of Mal-development in the North: A Way Out, *International Foundation for Development Alternatives* (IFDA), Dossier 2, pp. 1–11.

Sethi, Rajesh. 1982. 'Impact of Sectoral Change on Social Structure: A Study of a New Town,' Thesis submitted to Panjab University, unpublished.

Sharda, Bam Dev. 1977. *Status Attainment in Rural India*, Delhi, Ajanta Publications.

Sovani, N. V., D.P. Apte and R.G. Pendse. 1956. *Poona: A Resurvey*, Pune, Gokhale Institute of Politics and Economics, publication no. 34.

UNESCO. 1982. *Different Theories and Practices of Development*, Paris.

Index